What Was It?!

What Was It?!

A Short Guide to Understanding and Using Linux,
Macintosh and Windows—and Other Stuff

Henry Leach, Jr.

iUniverse, Inc.
New York Lincoln Shanghai

What Was It?!
A Short Guide to Understanding and Using Linux, Macintosh and Windows—and Other Stuff

iUniverse, Inc.

For information address:
iUniverse, Inc.
2021 Pine Lake Road, Suite 100
Lincoln, NE 68512
www.iuniverse.com

ISBN: 0-595-30915-1

Printed in the United States of America

Contents

PART V: DATA SAVED

PART VI: MAKING CHOICES

Preface

Computer technology is constantly evolving. The potential to change the way we live, work, and interact is increasingly determined by processors, bits and bytes, ones and zeroes. Soon our refrigerators will be able to communicate with us, informing us that the milk, eggs, and butter are running low. Better yet, we will be able to customize the refrigerator to prompt us should we buy a particular food item with fat instead of without.

Because technology is in constant flux, a computer manual is only as good as the current technology—the here and now. This book will serve as a guide to help you to:

- Ask the right questions when buying a computer, hardware, software, printer, etc.
- Learn where computer technology is headed.
- Change a setting or settings on your computer, if necessary.
- Determine which operating systems are best for performing certain tasks.
- Identify the printer that is best suited to the needs of a home office user.

Even as technology and its functionality evolve, however, we can take some solace in the fact that many of its core attributes are preserved. This should make the evolutionary process somewhat smoother.

For better or worse, we are all affected by computer technology. Cash registers, credit cards, ATM machines, cell phones, etc. All rely on processors, bits and bytes, ones and zeroes to move and analyze data.

Early in my career, I accepted a position as a computer support/tech equipment purchaser. I knew little about computer technology, but I was eager to learn and spent many hours reading technology books and visiting web sites. Most important, I practiced the things I was learning and learned from my mistakes, and in so doing, acquired an extensive knowledge of computer technology. Beginning then, and in the ensuing years, I have learned a great deal about computers. I am truly grateful that my boss during that time, John Eric Langdale, gave me a chance.

As a technical support person primarily for computers running Windows and Macintosh operating systems, I have tested and used the techniques outlined in this book both on the job and at home. My goal here is to provide basic information. Many troubleshooting steps and techniques are not covered because they go well beyond the scope of this book. I have, however, included troubleshooting tips and information on my web site, which will be operational soon. My web address is: www.whatwasit.net. The name comes from the question that almost every computer user asks after the technical support person solves a problem: "What was it?" You may have asked the same question yourself on occasion.

Over the past three years, after advising and supporting consumers in the purchase of nearly $1 million of computer equipment, including desktops, workstations, laptops, servers, printers, scanners, monitors, digital cameras, memory, software, and various other accessories and peripherals, I have become very familiar with the problems that can occur. That experience has prompted me on more than one occasion to say, Thank goodness for the warranties!

I could not have completed this book without invaluable help from the online community who were my references for most of the information presented here. For their subject knowledge and foresight, I would like to express my thanks to the people behind the following web sites.

about.com
activewin.com
apdirectory.com
apple.com
amd.com
a special thanks to CNET.com, whose editorial on purchasing computer equipment and peripherals provided critical information for **Part VI Making Choices**
cdwg.com, with their monthly educational literature on computer technology;
computerhope.com
dell.com, for making such a reliable product with excellent technical support; epinions.com
extremetech.com, with their insight on emerging technology;
gnu.org.
intel.com
ieee.org, the true wireless standard leaders;
jsifaq.com
linuxnovice.org., for making Linux easy to master;
lycos.com, where you can learn almost anything computer-related;
microsoft.com
motorola.com
nodedb.com, where wireless is just a click away;
nero.com
o'reily.com
pcguide.com, which provides detailed and outstanding information on computers; redhat.com

roxio.com
sophos.com, for their quick online virus scanner and their clear and easily navigated web site;
sandpile.org
siliconvalley.com
symantec.com
toaster.net
webopedia.com, with their encyclopedic technology database; and
80211-planet.com.

Thank you all.

Thanks Mom and Dad.

Thanks Guai Guai.

Henry Leach, Jr.

Introduction

This book is designed to provide as much detail as possible to help the user grasp basic computer concepts. Keep in mind, however, that due to incompatible operating systems, third party software, and user error, not all techniques will work flawlessly as described. Yet it is my hope that everyone who reads this book will benefit from the information presented and, ultimately, will find the computing experience less stressful and less fearful.

We begin with basic concepts such as the Desktop and types of operating systems and move on to more advanced topics such as command prompt commands, formatting a hard drive, and installing an operating system.

This book is for anyone who wishes to better understand computer technology—from beginners looking to purchase computer equipment and peripherals, to users who wish to learn a few advanced techniques, to the more advanced user who may be considering changes in his or her system or perhaps switching to a new operating system.

In each chapter, Windows and Macintosh techniques are described in a sequential format. This should minimize the need to refer to earlier or later chapters to obtain the same information. Although Linux is placed in a chapter by itself, many of the same techniques described for Windows and Macintosh are applicable.

Enjoy.

PART I
The Core of The Box

1

The Desktop

The Desktop is the background that has your personalized **wallpaper** or screen image and the various icons placed either by you or the system software. The Desktop can be seen when all windows you are working on are minimized. The various desktops appear below.

THE WINDOWS (PC) DESKTOP

On the Windows (PC) Desktop, you will find the **My Computer** icon, the **My Network Places** icon, and the **Taskbar** (the gray horizontal bar at the bottom containing the **Start** button).

THE MACINTOSH DESKTOP (OS X)

On the **OS X** Desktop you will find the **Apple icon** (in the top left corner), the **Hard Drive icon** (labeled on this picture as OS10.2.2, though yours may have a different name), and **The Dock** (at the bottom of the picture containing different icons).

NOTE: The little black arrows indicate the programs that are running.

THE MACINTOSH DESKTOP (OS 9)

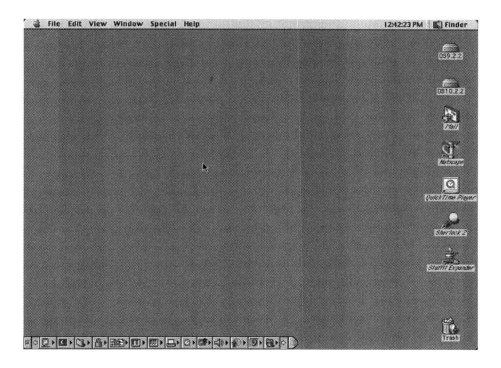

On the **OS 9** Desktop you will find the **Apple icon** (in the top left corner), the **Hard Drive icon** (labeled on this picture as OS9.2.2, though your hard drive may have a different name), and the **Control Strip** (at the bottom of the Desktop showing different icons).

NOTE: The control strip can be moved by holding down the Control key and moving the strip up or down with your mouse.

RED HAT DESKTOP

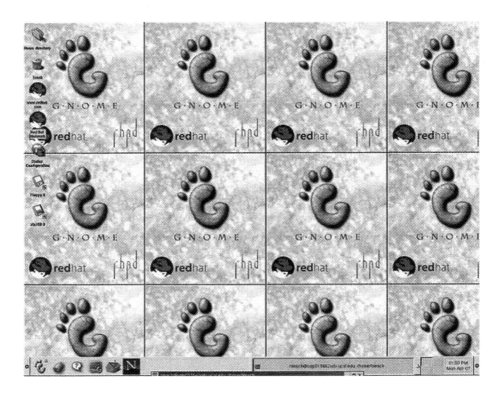

The **Red Hat Linux** Desktop layout is similar to the Windows Desktop layout. At the bottom of the Desktop there is the taskbar with the **Start Button** in the likeness of an **Animal Paw**. Instead of the My Computer icon, however, there is the **Home Directory** icon. Similar to a Macintosh, any external devices such as the CD ROM or Zip Drive are found on the Desktop.

NOTE: This is the Desktop wallpaper I picked from the numerous choices available.

2

Operating Systems

	Windows 95	Windows 98	Windows 98 SE	Windows NT	Windows 2000
Recommended Processor	386DX	66MHz	66MHz	33MHz	133MHz
Recommended Memory	4 MB	16 MB	24 MB	32MB	64 MB
Recommended Hard Drive	35 MB	195 MB	205 MB	110 MB	650 MB
The Bad	Few Powerful Features No Security Only Supports FAT and FAT-32	Lacking Major Security Features Only Support FAT and FAT-32	Lacking Major Security Features Only Supports FAT and FAT-32	Can be Difficult to Install Has Hard Drive Size Limitation Lacks Support for USB and Various Devices	Requires More Memory and a Fast Processor to get the Full benefits of the System
The Good	Auto Detection of New Devices Does Not Require a Powerful Computer	Supports DVD, USB, MMX Auto Detection of New Devices	Includes Major Fixes and Patches from Earlier Version	Advanced Security Features Advanced Multitasking Supports FAT and NTFS Supports 4 Processors	Fewer Crashes Multi-language Support Supports a Wide-range of Devices and Software Supports all File Systems Supports 2 Processors

	Windows ME	Windows XP	Mac OS 9	Mac OS X
Recommended Processor	150MHz	233MHz	Power PC	PowerPC G3
Recommended Memory	64MB	128MB	40 MB	128 MB
Recommended Hard Drive	410MB	1.5 GB	32 MB	1.5GB
The Bad	Can Crash More Often Does Not have a Wide-range of Software Compatibility	Requires More Memory, Fast Processor and Big Hard Drive to get the Full Benefits of the System XP Home Edition is not a good choice for corporate networks	Frequent System Crashes Lack of Software and Hardware Compatibility	Requires More Memory, Fast Processor and Big Hard Drive To Install Uses UNIX as the Main System, may be difficult to Troubleshoot Somewhat Limited Software and Hardware Compatibility
The Good	Good for Multimedia, Gaming and Movie Editing Can Restore the System with The Touch of a Button if Problems occur.	Very Stable Fast Startup and Shutdown Universal Hardware Support Built-in Firewall Supports 2 Processors	Relatively Easy to Learn and Troubleshoot Problems Fast Startup and Shutdown Excellent Multimedia Support Supports 4 Processors	Very Powerful and Stable System Very Little System Crashes Advanced Multitasking Advanced Security Features

WINDOWS LONGHORN

In 2005, Microsoft is set to release **Windows Longhorn**. This will be a non-server operating system. The next server release by Microsoft is scheduled for a few years after Longhorn.

Longhorn is expected to feature a new database file system that will be known as **Windows Future Storage (WinFS)**. Microsoft's Trustworthy Computing will be a major focus under Longhorn, and will feature overall system and software security. In addition, finding files and system information will be made easier and 3D rendering technology will deliver a richer visual appearance.

Microsoft's **Palladium** security standard will debut within the Longhorn operating system. This package, which involved both software developers and chip makers, is designed to set the stage for the complete rebuilding of the PC. Also, it is said that the Palladium standard will eliminate viruses and spam and offer greater user privacy.

UNIX AND LINUX

Although **Unix** and **Linux** have many things in common, they are two very different systems. Unix is not an acronym. Rather it is a play on words from an older time-sharing operating system called Multrics. Unix was originally designed for a single user environment, hence "U"nix. Linux (*li'nuks*) was started in 1991 by Linus Torvalds, a college student collaborating with developers throughout the world who wanted to use an operating system other than Windows. Linux is very Unix-like, but has no ties with Unix. From the beginning, Linux was part of the **General Public License (GPL)** system in which changes to the system (or kernel) can be distributed, used, and expanded free of charge. With this open source, access problems in the programming code (i.e., "bugs") could be found and quickly eliminated. Unix, however, has more controlled releases and is developed in a controlled, structured manner. All security-related changes to the system (kernel) must undergo peer review before a change is made.

Although Unix and Linux are by far the most stable and reliable operating systems, newcomers may find them difficult to use.

Computer Requirements	Runs on Virtually any Computer	Runs on a variety of Different Computers Depending on Distribution Chosen
Number of Different Distributions	17	100 and counting
Most Popular Distribution	BSD Unix	Red Hat Linux and SuSE
Advantages	Free	Free
	Supports Less New Hardware	Supports More and Newer Hardware and Has a Larger Share of Users
	Can be Used on Very Old Computers	
		Very Solid, Stable and Powerful
	Very Solid, Stable and Powerful	
		Allows for Changes to be Made to the Software
	Geared Toward Quality	
Disadvantages	Has a More Strict Set of Guidelines If Changes are Made to the Source Code	May be more Difficult to Learn for the Windows and Macintosh OS User
	May be More Difficult to Learn for the Windows and Macintosh OS User	
Special Features	Used on Some of The Most Advanced Computer Systems in the World	Used on Some of The Most Advanced Computer Systems In The World

3

Computer Processors

WHAT QUALIFIES AS A TRULY FAST COMPUTER?

The speed with which a web page loads is not a measure of actual computer speed. Web page loading is contingent upon an external process, i.e., the network speed that you are using (56K Modem, Cable, DSL, LAN). Thus, the true test of computer speed comes when you take away the network component and use the computer exclusively for processor-intensive work.

Manufacturers and tech gurus measure a computer's speed by its processor. The processor's performance is measured by its capacity to calculate **integers** and, more important, **floating-point variables**. Integers are numbers without decimal points including 1, 2, 3,-590834675, etc. They are easier for the computer processor to work with and take much less memory to store; however, for the computer technology industry, the better a processor is at calculating floating-point numbers the higher the speed that can be attributed to that processor. Floating-point numbers have decimal points such as 1.3, 4998.43,-.092, 44.56, etc. To calculate these numbers, a computer processor usually has to work much harder. In addition, it takes more memory to store floating-point numbers. Programs that use floating-points include Computer Aided Design (CAD), 3D rendering/ modeling, animation, video games, special effect filters, and scientific applications. Processors made by AMD, the Itanium processor made by Intel and Hewlett-Packard, and the Macintosh processor made by IBM specialize in this sort of number crunching This is one reason why people in the multimedia industry choose a Macintosh.

MULTIPROCESSOR

The theory behind a **multiprocessor** is that you can double performance by using two processors instead of one. The reality is that it does not work that way, although multiprocessing can result in improved performance.

Multiprocessing is most effective when used with application software designed specifically for it. A **threaded** application is designed to use more than one processor and is broken into smaller streams that can be run independently. The operating system then allows these threads to run on more than one processor simultaneously, thus improving performance. If the application is not designed this way, it cannot take advantage of multiple processors.

In summary, if the software you are using does not support two processors, only one processor will be used and the other will sit idle. If you intend to use specialized software with your computer, check with the software company beforehand to determine if the software is multiprocessor aware.

THE PC PROCESSORS
THE INTEL PENTIUM

	Pentium	Pentium Pro	Pentium w/MMX	Pentium II	Celeron	Pentium III
CPU Speed	60-66MHz	133-200MHz	166-233MHz	233-450MHz	300-2GHz	500-1GHz
L2 Cache	256-512KB (on board)	256-1MB (on board)	256-512KB	512KB	128KB	256KB
L3 Cache	NONE	NONE	NONE	NONE	NONE	NONE
Bus Speed	33MHz	60-66MHz	66MHz	100MHz	66MHz	100MHz &133MHz
Calculate Floating Point Numbers	Good	Good	Strong	Strong	Strong	Strong
Calculate Integers	Strong	Strong	Strong	Strong	Strong	Strong
Uses	Desktops	Desktops	Desktops and Laptops	Desktops and Laptops	Desktops and Laptops	Desktops and Laptops

(Pentium Continued)

	Pentium 4	Pentium Xeon	Pentium Itanium 2	Pentium 5
CPU Speed	1.4GHz –over 2GHz	500MHz-over 2GHz	1GHz and Beyond	4 to 5GHz and Beyond
L2 Cache	256KB	256-2MB	1.5MB	??
L3 Cache	NONE	NONE	3MB	??
Bus Speed	533MHz	100MHz-533MHz	400MHz	??
Calculate Floating Point Numbers	Strong	Strong	Excellent	??
Calculate Integers	Strong	Strong	Excellent	??
Uses	Desktops and Laptops	Mostly Servers and High-end Desktops	Servers and Advanced Systems	Servers and Desktops

THE AMD ATHLON

	AMD K6	AMD K6-II	AMD K6-III	AMD Duron	AMD Athlon K7
CPU Speed	166-300MHz	500-550MHz	400-450MHz	700-800MHz	850-1.2GHz
L2 Cache Bus Speed	256 onboard 66 & 100MHz	256 KB onboard 100MHz	256 KB onboard 100MHz	64 KB 200MHz	512 KB 200 & 266MHZ
Calculate Floating Points	Good	Strong	Weak	Very Strong	Very Strong
Calculate Integers	Strong	Strong	Excellent	Strong	Very Strong
Uses	Desktops	Desktops and Laptops	Desktops and Laptops	Desktops, Laptops and Servers	Desktops, Laptops and Servers

(AMD Continued)

	AMD Athlon XP	AMD 4 (Opteron)
CPU Speed	1.47-over 2GHz	1.6GHz to over 3GHz
L2 Cache	384 KB	Up to 1MB
Bus Speed	266MHz	333MHz and Above
Calculate Floating Points	Excellent	????
Calculate Integers	Excellent	????
Uses	Desktops, Laptops and Servers	High-end Desktops and Servers

THE MACINTOSH PROCESSORS
THE MOTOROLA POWERPC

	PowerPC 750 G3	PowerPC G3	PowerPC G4	PowerPC 7450 G4	PowerPC 7500 or 8500 G5
CPU Speed	233-266MHz	300-450MHz	350-500MHz	733-over 1GHz	800MHz to over 2.4GHz
L2 Cache	512KB	1MB Backside	1MB Backside	256KB	128KB – 512KB
L3 Cache	None	None	None	2MB	???
Bus Speed	66MHz	66-100MHz	100MHz	133MHz	400MHz
Calculate Floating Point Numbers	Very Strong	Very Strong	Excellent	Excellent	Excellent
Calculate Integers	Very Strong	Very Strong	Excellent	Excellent	Excellent
Uses	Desktops	Desktops and Laptops	Desktops, Laptops and Servers	Desktops, Laptops and Servers	Desktops and Servers

CHECK YOUR COMPUTER'S PROCESSOR SPEED

Using a PC: Start up the computer. Press the **F2** key (the key(s) the system requires to enter system setup) to go into the **System BIOS** where you will find the information.

Another way is to click the **Start** button. Go to **Control Panel. Administrative Tools, Computer Management**. Choose **System Information** and check the **Processor** information to see the processor speed in **MHz**.

With **Windows XP**, right-click the **My Computer** icon and scroll to **Properties**. You will see the Processor speed in MHz.

Using a Macintosh: Go to the **Apple** icon and scroll to **About This Computer**. You will see the processor information of the Mac in MHz.

4

Random Access Memory (RAM)

RAM is the electronic substance that will determine what you can and cannot accomplish while using a computer. When you open or start an application (Word, Excel, etc.) that application in turn occupies space in RAM, which then renders that portion of the RAM unavailable. As more and more applications are started, more and more spots in RAM are filled. When you open more applications than the computer has memory to store, an "out of memory" error may occur.

While a computer is running, it uses its memory to hold the programs with which you are working (e.g., Word, Excel, Netscape), the operating system files, the music player you are using, etc. Essentially, everything that is running on the computer will take up a space in memory. To find out what applications are being held in memory on a Windows (PC), press **Ctrl+Alt+Delete.** Under the **processes** tab you will see all of the running processes, the amount of memory each takes up, and how much of the processor each uses. With more memory, the computer can work on more tasks more efficiently. For example, someone creating Photoshop images will have bigger memory requirements than someone using simple word processing and sending electronic mail (e-mail). So, the amount of memory you need is based on the tasks you intend to perform. In the computer world, however, a widely accepted maxim when it comes to RAM is: The more the better!

When a computer's memory is too low to handle the programs with which you are working, you will receive an "out of memory message." Although most users do not reach the maximum capacity of their computer's memory, users working with large images may encounter this problem occasionally. The problem can be addressed in one of two ways. Either close some of the images or add more memory.

Paging File/Virtual Memory—PC

Your computer also uses a **paging file**, an area on the hard drive used as if it were RAM. When the computer's memory runs low, it uses the paging file to store the data that can no longer fit in memory. The Windows operating system usually sets the paging file size automatically based on the amount of RAM in the system; however, advanced users can change this setting to meet their needs. The paging file setting can be adjusted by going to **Start, Settings, Control Panel, System, Advanced**.

NOTE: You will not be able to adjust the setting to a value that is beyond the scope of the system.

PAGING FILE/VIRTUAL MEMORY—OS 9

Go to the **Apple icon**, **Control Panel, Memory**. Enable **Virtual Memory**, if not already enabled. The operating system will automatically set the appropriate amount of Virtual Memory to use. You can also adjust the amount of Virtual Memory used by OS 9.

PAGING FILE/VIRTUAL MEMORY—OS X

There is no paging file/virtual memory feature available for OS X.

CHECKING YOUR COMPUTER'S MEMORY

Using a PC—Go to the Desktop and right-click the **My Computer** icon. You will be presented with a selection box. Scroll down to **Properties**. You will then see information about your computer including the amount of memory ink **kilobytes (Kb)**. Multiply this number by **1024** to get the number in **megabytes (MB)**. A few examples and their approximate values include:

128MB = 130,382KB
256MB = 260,764KB
384MB = 391,148KB
512MB = 521,529KB
640MB = 651,911KB
768MB = 782,294KB
896MB = 912,676KB
1GB = 1,043,058KB

bytes, kilobytes, megabytes, and gigabytes
1 byte (b) = 1 character
1 kilobyte (Kb) = 1024 bytes
1 megabyte (MB) = 1024 KB = 1,048,576 bytes
1 gigabyte (GB) = 1024 MB = 1,048,576 KB = 1,073,741,824 bytes

Another way to view the memory information is to start up the computer, press the **F2** key (to enter **system setup**), go into the **System BIOS**—area of computer detailing system information and settings that may be changed.

<u>Using a Macintosh</u>—Across the top of the desktop, go to the **Apple icon** and scroll to **About This Computer**.

THE MEMORY CHIP (RAM CHIP)

The **Memory Chip** is a small wafer of silicon etched with thousands of integrated electronic circuits that carry and hold data instructions. The wafers are stacked in layers and covered with a protective material resulting in what are called "chips". The memory chip is the actual material that holds the RAM. Think of the memory chip as the cup and the RAM as the liquid in the cup. Keep in mind that RAM and Memory will be used interchangeably.

DIFFERENT TYPES OF MEMORY

RAM comes in different flavors to meet the needs of the computer in which it will be used, the below chart details this information.
NOTE: You cannot always mix memory from different makes of computer systems.

Memory can be classified as **Error Correction Code** (ECC)**,** which corrects memory errors. This is useful for servers. **Non-ECC** is standard memory without the error correction. This type of memory is found in most computers. Overall, non-ECC memory will suit most computing needs. **Parity** is another form of error correction code that was used in older memory chips.

Memory can also be classified by the **bus speed** (or **clock speed**) it supports. The bus speed is the speed at which the processor sends information to and from memory. A **bus** is a collection of wires through which data is transmitted from one part of a computer to another. Common memory bus speeds include PC-66 or 66MHz, PC-100 or 100MHz, and PC-133 or 133MHz. Thus, data is shuttled in and out of the memory at speeds of 66, 100 or 133MHz, respectively.

MOVING DATA

In computers, data moves from the hard drive to RAM and then to the processor. Since the processor is faster than RAM, and RAM is faster than the hard drive, computers need **cache**—pronounced *cash*—to help the slower data meet the faster data. A cache is a temporary storage location for previously used data. Cache feeds information as needed as fast as possible. First, the computer looks in the **L1** Cache to see if the information is there. If the information is not there, then it looks in the **L2** Cache. Finally, it will look in the **L3** Cache, if the computer supports an L3 Cache. If the computer does not find the information there, it goes to the RAM. Finally, if the information is not found in the RAM, the computer goes to the hard drive. As you can see, a computer is designed to gain access to data as quickly as possible. It does so through a process of elimination, taking the fastest route (L1 Cache) to the slowest (hard drive). Have you ever noticed that you can still read a web page even after you have become disconnected from the Internet? The reason for this is caching.

Chart of RAM

	ROM	EDO	SDRAM	RDRAM
Name	Read Only Memory	Extended Data Out	Synchronous Dynamic Random Access Memory	Rambus Dynamic Random Access Memory
Clock Speed	4.7MHz	33-75MHz	PC 66MHz PC 100MHz PC 133MHz PC150MHz	200-800MHz
Data Transfer Rate	Fixed	266Mbps	800Mbps – 1.28Gbps	1.6Gbps
Number of PINS	N/A	72	144 & 168	168 (non-ECC) 184 (ECC)
Types Available	Standard	SIMM	SODIMM & DIMM	RIMM
Can be Used in Desktops	Standard	Yes	Yes	Yes
Can be Used in Laptops	Standard	No	Yes	No
Supports ECC	No	Supports Parity	Yes	Yes
Memory Latency	None	Low	Low	High
Special Features	Only Keeps Information that Start Computer	Older Memory That is no Longer used	The Current Industry Standard	Rather Expensive and Not Compatible with Any other Memory Has a high Latency

(RAM Continued)

	DDR	NDRAM
Name	Double Data Rate Dynamic Access Ram	Proposed Future version of RDRAM
Clock Speed	200-300MHz	1,600MHz
Data Transfer Rate	1.6 – 2.7 Gbps	1.6 – 3.0Gbps
Number of PINS	184	N/A
Types Available	DIMM & SODIMM	N/A
Can be Used in Desktops	Yes	N/A
Can be Used in Laptops	Yes	N/A
Supports ECC	Yes	N/A
Memory Latency	Low	N/A
Special Features	Could Soon Replace SDRAM and RDRAM	Under Development by Intel and Rambus, Inc

USB MEMORY STICK

The newest advance in technology is the **USB powered transportable memory drive**. This device, which is the size of a pen, connects to a computer's USB port. Any sort of data, including programs, can be stored on these devices provided there is enough room. Unlike regular memory, which loses information the moment the power is switched off, the memory stick keeps its data until you erase it. Data can be saved to these devices and erased up to 1 million times. Sizes vary from as little as 16MB to as high as 2GB. Most of the devices are supported by all major operating systems Windows (except Windows NT4.0), Macintosh, and Linux

5

Computer Systems and Servers

Below is a list of various computer systems. The list is for information only. In the list, I have given more attention to the **server.**

I.   DESKTOP COMPUTER

This is the most common type of computer system and is used by most consumers for general tasks at work and at home. The desktop computer contains fewer costly components and features.

II.   PORTABLE COMPUTER (LAPTOP)

This is the transportable version of the desktop computer.

III.   WORKSTATION

This is a more powerful version of the desktop computer.

IV.   SERVER

This is a computer used to 'serve' data for others to access. It provides Internet serving, intranet serving, print serving, file serving, web site serving, etc. These computers are rapidly replacing the mainframe.

V.   MAINFRAME

These are large centralized computers good for large-scale tasks involving centralized billing systems, inventory systems, and database operation. Mainframes are becoming less common.

VI.   RENDER FARM/SERVER FARM

These are collections of computers that work together to render (produce) processor intensive calculations for special effects or web hosting.

VII.   CLUSTER

This is the cheaper version of a supercomputer capable of billions of calculations per second. Clusters can perform many of the same tasks as the supercomputer.

VIII.   SUPERCOMPUTER

A supercomputer is primarily used for processes requiring extremely fast, error-free speeds for scientific computing, stock trading systems, and processing credit card transactions. The web site **Google.com** uses a supercomputer as a server running the Linux operating system with about 100,000 processors and 261,000 hard drives (and growing). This is reported to be the largest supercomputer in the world, efficiently handling 200 million searches per day, at a relatively fast speed. Supercomputers are capable of billions of calculations of data per second and are by far the fastest, most advanced, and most costly computers.

Servers comprise a significant portion of the computers we use at work and while accessing the Internet. Once folders, files, and/or printers are shared on a computer, that computer acts as a server.

COMMON SERVER OPERATING SYSTEMS

	Windows	Novell Netware	Linux
Overview	Provides an easy-to-learn network base that can be administered with a minimum of specialized technical knowledge.	Provides more control over a network for experienced network administrators.	Excellent for large-scale networking and Intranet, FTP, E-mail and File Storage applications.
Advantages	Good for Basic Server needs like File Servers, Internet access control, FTP. Does not Require Extensive Technical Knowledge. Makes Server Tasks Easier than other server-based systems. Widely Used Throughout the World Compatible with Most Software on the Market.	Was designed solely for network server use, using a system that can be easily administered and organized. Long history on the server market. Most casual users will not be able to circumvent its security measures or commit malicious acts.	Very versatile and powerful providing the maximum server capability to experienced network administrators. Can be run on low-end computer hardware. Upgrades to every aspect of the system are free to download and install. Employs a very powerful security model.
Disadvantages	Biggest Target of Hackers and Virus Writers. Upgrades can be costly and Problematic	Uses Proprietary network technology that will increase overall cost.	Less widely known to casual computer users. Developers often overlook Linux when designing software and hardware.

PART II
Systems in Effect

6

Choosing a Computer

Choosing a computer can be difficult given the various brands, costs, features, and add-ons. The following information—call it "food for thought"—might help to ease some of the confusion and difficulty inherent to the process of buying a computer.

MACINTOSH OR WINDOWS?

Things to consider: Cost, Compatibility, Ease of Use, Performance, and Style.
NOTE: Mac will refer to computers using Macintosh operating system and PC will refer to computers using the Windows operating system.

Cost: Look at your budget and determine what you can afford. Some of the nicely equipped entry-level Macintosh computers tend to be more expensive than many of the entry-level Windows PCs that are also nicely equipped.

Compatibility: Since the majority of the computers in the world run under the Windows platform, it will be much easier to integrate whatever you are doing with a Windows PC. For adding new hardware, software, or replacement parts, the PC is more versatile than the Mac.

Ease of Use: The buzzword "user-friendly" has been used to describe the Macintosh. With the introduction of the **Graphical User Interface** (**GUI**) by Xerox PARC, making use of icons and folders, both PCs and Macs can be user-friendly. Today, both PC and Mac use the GUI model.

Performance: There is still debate as to whether a PC is better and faster than a Mac and vice versa. The best way to answer this question is to judge how well each platform performs the same tasks. Macs tend to perform better on multimedia-oriented tasks, e.g., using the Adobe Software suite (Photoshop in particular.) Although PCs, especially those equipped with the AMD processor, can perform similar tasks well, Mac remains a proven winner. Yet if you are an avid video game user (gamer) you will want to go with a PC. There are far more games built for the PC. Macs do tend to crash quite often, in particular under the OS 9 operating system. Fortunately, with the release of OS X, the new Unix-based operating system for the Mac, crashes are rare, and you get Unix to work with.

Standard Features: On average, Macintosh computers tend to have more standard features than the PC, which probably accounts for the premium price. FireWire ports, USB ports, Digital Video ports, Gigabit Ethernet, CD-RW/DVD-RW combo Drive, just to name a few, are standard on most Macintosh computers. Although some of these features are becoming available as standard equipment on the PC, other features remain available only as costly add-ons.

Advanced Technology: Most computers made today (in particular the Macintosh) are on the cutting-edge of technology. The majority of today's supercomputers, however, are based on the PC platform.

Reliability: Both the Macs and the PCs have reliability issues. Hard drives go bad, motherboards stop functioning, memory become problematic, etc. Keep in mind that the parts of a computer are not made by the computer manufacturer, but rather by a third party vendor. It is the responsibility of the manufacturer to ensure that only quality parts from quality vendors go into their computers. Although the Macintosh usually contains high quality components, as of this writing they are experiencing major problems. PC vendors, such as Dell, carry top brand parts as well. Bottom line? When it comes to buying a computer, the old adage "you get what you pay for" rings especially true.

Style: Without question the makers of the Macintosh computer are the leaders in computer design and style, with their various colors and shapes and use of lightweight materials. Although Macintosh computers are by far some of the most visually pleasing and powerful computers, in many instances practicality and functionality have been sacrificed in favor of style. Currently, the Macintosh is receiving low marks for structural integrity.

Computer Viruses: Most computers in use today run on the PC platform, and there are more viruses that take advantage of that fact. Viruses written for Macs are, for the moment, rare; however, if there is a substantial jump in Mac ownership (witness the increasing popularity of the OS X), this could change. The PC will probably always be susceptible to viruses of some sort due to ubiquity of the Windows operating systems.

Other factors to consider when making a computer purchase

- Available Computer Warranties
- Reliability of the Brand
- Level of Technical Support Available
- How Quickly the Company Resolves Repair Problems

What Do The Choices Mean?

There are a lot of different choices when configuring a computer. Many computer manufacturers offer a pre-set bundled package. Others allow you to custom-build your computer. When buying a computer look for Processor, Display, Memory, Hard Drive, Optical Drive, Graphics Card, Modem/NIC, Sound, Software, Warranty, and Installation Support.

Processors: Some vendors will have the Intel Celeron and the Pentium III or Pentium 4 to choose from. Currently, most desktop computers are shipped with Pentium 4 processors, and it is probably best to get the Pentium 4 to keep up with the latest technological trends. Although the Celeron has some caching limitations, the 1.5GHz and over Celeron processors could be a worthy choice. Still, if you can afford it, go with the Pentium.

Another term used with reference to processors is the **MHz** or **GHz** number. This describes the speed of the processor. Most Pentium 4 processors have at least 1GHz. This component of the computer changes from month to month. For general use, you will not notice a profound difference in the speed of a system with a 1GHz processor compared to a 1.5GHz processor. So, get what you can afford, keeping in mind that more is not always better, especially for general computer use (i.e., word processing, e-mail, web surfing, etc.)

Remember also that by the time you get your computer, unpack it, and turn it on, it is already close to obsolescence. Computer technology changes constantly. Waiting for prices to go down before you buy could mean waiting forever, as there is negative correlation between price and evolving technology—it becomes cheaper as it evolves.

Display

- **Flat Screen:** This is not the cutting-edge, space-saving monitor, as you might believe. Rather, the Flat Screen is a large, bulky CRT with a flat front.
- **Flat Panel/LCD:** This is the space-saving, thin monitor. They cost more, but you may decide that the savings in desk space and the ergonomic and energy-saving benefits make up for the higher price.
- **CRT:** This is the typical large monitor that takes up space.

Memory

When considering memory, buy as much as you can afford—the more the better.

- **ECC 1 DIMM:** The ECC 1 DIMM checks for memory errors. On a computer with 512MB of RAM, ECC 1 DIMM would occupy only one slot (1 DIMM). If you wanted to add memory in the future, you simply add it to the slot that is not used. **NOTE: ECC memory also comes in the 2 DIMMS format**.
- **Non-ECC 2 DIMMS:** In this configuration, the MB of RAM will be split in half and occupy two memory slots. Thus, in a computer with 512MB of RAM, there would be a 256MB chip

in one slot and a 256MB chip in the other slot. **NOTE: non-ECC memory is also available in the 1 DIMM format.**

Hard Drive: The size of the hard drive you choose will depend on how much data you plan to store. The more data you store, the bigger the hard drive you will need. A 40 to 80 GB hard drive is sufficient for most purposes; however, as the capacity of hard drives increase, the reliability of the drive decreases. Always back up data onto another device, e.g., a CD, DVD or another hard drive.

- **5400 RPM, 7200RPM(Ultra ATA), 10,000 RPM (Ultra SCSI), 15,000 RPM (Ultra SCSI):** These are the speeds at which the hard drive spins. The faster the speed, the faster the access to data on the hard drive—also the more expensive. The 7200 RPM (Ultra ATA) hard drive is sufficient for most desktops. If you deal with huge databases or crunch lots of data sets, however, 10,000 to 15,000 RPM SCSI hard drives would be preferable. For laptops, 3500 to 4500 RPM is acceptable, but if a higher speed is available consider purchasing it. It is always good to access to your data as quick as possible.

Optical Drive This includes the CD-ROM, DVD-ROM, CD-RW (CD Burner), and DVD-RW/+RW (DVD Burner).

- **48x Max. CD-ROM Drive:** In this configuration, the CD-ROM drive can read CDs at a maximum speed of 48x.

- **16x DVD-ROM Drive:** In this configuration, the DVD-ROM has a maximum speed of 16x and reads only DVDs and regular CDs.

- **24x/10x/40x CD-RW:** In this configuration, the CD burner can burn CD-R CDs at a speed of 24x, CD-RW CDs at 10x, and read regular CDs at a speed of 40x.

- **Combo Drive (CD-RW/DVD-ROM):** This is used by Apple to signify a CD-Burner combined with a DVD-ROM Drive.

- **Super Drive (CD-RW/DVD-RW):** This is used by Apple to signify a computer with a combined CD-Burner and DVD-Burner.

- **CD/RW and CD-ROM:** This is another configuration that gives you two drives. One drive will be able to read and write CDs. The other drive will be able to read CDs only. This configuration is useful for those who intend to copy disks.

- **DVD+RW/CD-RW:** This drive allows you to both burn data to DVD discs and CD-R discs, as well as read DVDs and CDs.

Graphics Card: (also called Video card) The video card helps accomplish brighter and crisper monitor resolutions, which are especially useful with LCD monitors. These can be helpful for DVD movies and games otherwise the standard graphics card will be good enough to suit your needs. The graphics card helps paint the image on the screen much faster, and due to the limiting fast-image technology of the LCD, this is useful.

- **64MB ATI Mobility RADEON:** This graphics card uses an ATI RADEON with 64MB of RAM.

- **128MB DDR NVIDIA GeForce with TV-Out and DVI:** This graphics card uses 128MB of DDR-RAM and has a port to connect to a television set and a port to connect a digital monitor.

- **Analog LCD Monitor:** This monitor uses an analog signal, which results in less than crisp images.

- **Digital LCD Monitor:** This monitor uses digital signals **(DVI),** which results in very crisp resolutions. In conjunction with a good graphics card and fast CPU, there is noticeable clarity and crispness when viewing or creating movies and games on the computer. Apple, by far, makes the most advanced digital monitors available to the average personal computer user.

Modem/Networking/Wireless Networking: Most computers come with a built-in modem and Network Interface Card (NIC). A new add-on for computers is the wireless card, which allows for wireless networking. Unless otherwise noted, these devices will be internal. When considering the wireless option, keep in mind that you will need a wireless base station to carry the signal. Usually, the base station must be purchased separately. Otherwise you can connect to existing wireless base stations at work, in coffeehouses, or access your neighbor's.

Sound: A sound card that allows you to listen to music on external speakers is standard equipment with most computers. As an alternative, you can purchase a more specialized sound card that provides more versatility, power, and noise reduction to enhance your multimedia experience. You can also purchase a computer with a speaker built in to the computer, however, the sound quality of these speakers is not always the best.

Operating System: On the PC, operating system choices are determined by Microsoft. Currently, **Windows 2000**, **Windows XP Home Edition**, and **Windows XP Professional** are the main choices. If these systems are new to you, go with Windows XP Professional. Before long most computers will only be sold with XP. In addition, Microsoft will discontinue extended support for Windows 98 and Windows NT 4.0.

Windows XP Home Edition: This system is not recommended if you intend to put it on your company's network. XP Home Edition does not support what is called Domain networking, which companies use to administer computers. For home use only, however, XP Home is ideal and as good as XP Professional.

Windows XP Professional: This is a very stable and very big system. It starts up and shuts down much faster that Windows 2000. Most software is compatible with the system. Adding new hardware to your system is simple since so many hardware drivers (software) are already built in. It can be customized to look and feel like Windows 2000, although XP has more powerful built-in features, including a built-in firewall, the capacity to allow another XP user to control your computer from a remote location, and built-in games that allows you to play interactively with another person on the Internet.
NOTE: Until software "bugs" are corrected, you can expect minor problems to occur.

Windows 2000: This is a very stable, powerful, and universal system, yet without all of the enhancements found on XP. Because Windows 2000 has been around longer, most of the bugs have been corrected.

Mac OS X (Jaguar and Panther): This is Apple's new Unix-based multitasking operating system. Jaguar includes the OS 10.2 operating system; and Panther includes the 10.3 operating system. With a high-resolution monitor it is a beautiful system to view. The fonts and colors are very sharp and life-like. There are many enhancements that were not available in the past. The Unix console is a good example, it allows you to execute Unix commands and write code. The system is stable and crashes are rare. This system is standard in Apple computers, whether iBook, Powerbook, iMac, or PowerMac. No choices here. If you are interested in the more powerful features available to OS X, be sure to download the **developer tools** included with the OS X install CD.

Microsoft Office Software

Many of the specially priced computers made for the home user come bundled with a great deal of unnecessary software that you may never use. Buy the least amount of software possible. Uninstall any software that you are unlikely to use. Which software packages you need will depend on what tasks you intend to perform with your computer. The Microsoft Office Suite, which includes Outlook, Word, Excel, Power Point, should be standard. **Office 2003** has many powerful features geared towards business productivity and security.

- **Office 2000/XP Standard:** Includes standard office programs—Word, Excel, Outlook, and Power Point.

- **Office 2000/XP Professional:** Includes Word, Excel, Outlook, Publisher, Access, Power-Point, and Small Business Tools.

- **Office 2000 Premium:** Includes Word, Excel, Outlook, Publisher, Small Business Tools, Access, PowerPoint, FrontPage, and PhotoDraw.

- **Office 2000 Small Business:** Includes Word, Excel, Outlook, Publisher, and Small Business Tools.

- **Office XP Developer:** Includes Word, Excel, Outlook, PowerPoint, Access, Office Developer and FrontPage.

- **Office 2001 Mac:** This software is available for computers running the Macintosh OS. The package includes Word, PowerPoint, Entourage (an e-mail program), and Excel. Microsoft offers Outlook 2001 for the Mac as a separate and free download.

NOTE: Office 2001 Mac does not work with OS X.

- **Office X:** This software distribution is available only for Macintosh computers running OS X. Included with this distribution are Word, Excel, Entourage (e-mail program), and Power-Point.

Warranty

Although most computer makers offer a free one-year warranty and a 30-day return policy, it is a good idea to purchase additional coverage in the event you experience hardware failure after the original warranty expires. With extended coverage, you can call in for help with computer problems, and if needed, you will be sent a new part free of charge. Remember that most insurance only covers hardware (CD-ROM/CD-RW, hard drives, memory, keyboards, etc.) problems that arise from normal wear and tear. Although unexpected drops, liquid spills, or other acts of user carelessness are not covered in the standard warranty, you should ask if extra coverage is available for these types of mishaps. For example, **Dell** offers **Complete Care Coverage**, which includes damage incurred should you drop the computer or spill liquid into it.
NOTE: Theft is not covered.

Apple offers **AppleCare,** which covers most hardware-related problems for an additional three years. **Again, theft is not covered**.

Most computer manufacturers do not cover software problems unless they were already in the computer when it was shipped. Check with the computer vendor for more information about warranties and what is covered under the warranty.

LAPTOPS

Laptops are rapidly replacing the standard Desktop computer. In general, a laptop can perform the same functions as a desktop.

When choosing a laptop, the same issues should be taken into consideration as when choosing a desktop. Yet there are a few differences including the processor, screen resolution, battery choices, and port replicator option. In addition, if you opt for a laptop, be sure to buy an anti-theft lock as well as insurance against theft. This can sometimes be included in homeowners or renter's insurance policies. Consult your insurer. Macintosh Laptops since they have fewer choices available—iBook and PowerBook—I did not include them.

Laptop Processors

- **SpeedStep Technology:** Created by the Intel Corporation, this innovation allows the processor to reduce (or "step down") its speed whenever the laptop is using the battery for power. This feature can be enabled or disabled by the user.

- **Pentium III-m or Pentium 4-m:** With this feature, the laptop uses a Pentium chip, with technology optimized for better power management when the laptop is using the battery.

- **Pentium M:** This processor is designed for higher performance and low power consumption when using the battery. A built-in 1MBof L2 cache makes access to data much quicker. New features for laptops with the Pentium M processor include USB 2.0 ports and better wireless support.

- **Centrino Mobile Technology** or **Centrino:** This is comprised of the Pentium M processor and the PRO Wireless Connection Technology. The primary focus is wireless networking in laptops and tablet PCs, while incorporating all of the new features in the Pentium M. Soon all laptops will use the Pentium Centrino processor.

Screen Resolution

Pre-set screen resolutions optimized for the laptop are standard. For example, if you buy a laptop with a screen resolution advertised as 1,280 X 1,024, that will be the resolution that works best. Changing the resolution to a size different that what was purchased will result in fuzziness and a decrease in the sharpness of the resolution. Some laptop makers use the following codes to advertise screen resolutions:

- **SVGA**(800 x 600) This size is relatively large and not a standard option when buying a computer.

- **XGA**(1024 X 768) This is the standard screen resolution found on the less pricey or entry-level computers.

- **SXGA**(1280 X 1024) This resolution is good for data requiring high resolution.

- **UXGA**(1600 x 1200) A very high resolution. Text, fonts and graphics are very sharp and very small. If this is a choice, make sure at least 32MB of RAM video card is purchased.

- **Wide-aspect display** (Available in WXGA, WSXGA, WUXGA formats) This is the newest style of monitor available for PC laptops. It allows you to view more on the screen at once without making the image smaller. You can view two web pages side-by-side, two pages of a document, view more columns in a spreadsheet, and play games or watch DVD movies in their true format.

Laptop Batteries

If you intend to use your battery often, e.g., while in flight or in other regions where you would not have ready access to electricity, it is advisable to buy two batteries. Keep in mind that the more memory your computer has and the more devices you have connected to it (e.g., if you use the optical drive (CD-ROM/DVD-ROM) while using the battery), the faster the charge will be lost, since the battery would have to power all of those devices.

Port Replicator

This is a laptop plug-in device that provides an easy way to make a laptop feel like a desktop with ports for a full-sized keyboard, a mouse, and a monitor.

Wireless Card

If available, the wireless option should be considered. Airports, coffeehouses, Universities, homes, and businesses are going wireless. With a wireless card installed in your laptop, you will be able to connect to these wireless access points (some for a fee) and take part in regular web-related activities. If possible, choose the **internal** wireless card option.

Points to keep in mind when choosing a laptop

- Laptops are more expensive than desktops.

- Laptop parts can break down in demanding environments.

- Laptops are likely to be stolen, dropped, or damaged if the user is not very careful.

- It is advantageous to insure your laptop against theft. Most vendors do not sell theft insurance, so check with your insurance company or employer about laptop theft insurance policies.

Brands

When it comes to brands, there are plenty. Companies such as Dell, Apple, and IBM have better reputations in terms of quality and service. Other choices on the market include Sony, Compaq, Gateway, Hewlett-Packard, Toshiba, Asus, Acer and Chembook, just to name a few.

7

Monitors

There are two types of monitors: **cathode ray tube (CRT)** and **liquid crystal display (LCD)**. The **CRT** is the standard large desktop monitor to which many computer users are accustomed. These monitors have been around since the beginning of the computer revolution and have the same technology found in televisions. **LCD** (or Flat panel) monitors (or **TFT-LCD** for laptops) are rapidly becoming the standard. **Plasma** technology will one day occupy a bigger portion of this market. In the future, we will see plasma displays, also called **thin-panel displays**.

	CRT	LCD	PLASMA
Cost	Inexpensive	Expensive	Very Expensive
Common Sizes	12-inch to 21-inch	15-inch to 25-inch	15-inch to 60-inch
Advantages	Inexpensive Can Produce Images at Several Different Resolutions Has Best Overall Image Quality, especially with moving images	Brighter Picture, Sharper Images, Very Good Contrast. Low Power Consumption, Low Heat Output, Saves Desk Space, Eye-Strain and Headaches are Reduced Due to the Elimination of Screen Flicker	Brighter Than a LCD Offers a Very Wide Viewing Range Very Thin and Space-Saving Can Project Sharper Images Than a LCD
Disadvantages	Produces Heat Can Cause Eye-Strain and Headaches Screen Tends to Flicker Takes Up a Huge Amount of Space	Some Models Are not able to Produce Sharp Images at Different Resolutions Non-working pixels—"void pixels"—can Cause Permanent Faded Spots on the Screen	The Life Span is Determined by How Often The Display is Used Require the User to Use with Proper Care to Ensure Longevity Loses Brightness With Use and Age Very Expensive

DISPLAY RESOLUTIONS

Resolution	*Pixel Resolution*
Video Graphics Array (**VGA**)	640 x 480
SuperVGA (**SVGA**)	800 x 600
Extended Graphics Array (**XGA**)	1024 x 768
SuperXGA (**SXGA**)	1280 x 1024
UltraXGA (**UXGA**)	1600 x 1200
High-Definition TV (**HDTV**)	1920 x 1080
QuadXGA (**QXGA**)	2048 x 1536

PART III
Networking with Wires or No Wires

8

The Network

A **Network** is basically a collection of computers, printers, and servers sharing information. Being connected to a network allows individuals to share printers, faxes, scanners, hard drives, or any device connected to a networked computer. Most important, a network allows for rapid, cost-effective communication via **e-mai**l.

When your computer is added to a network it is given a name and IP address so that it can be identified within the network. Adding a computer to a network allows the user to share the resources available on that network including data, printers, software, e-mail, and the ability to save important data to specified servers. The new user receives a login name and a password so that he/she has authorization to access the network.

Depending on the type of network, an **IP address** is assigned to your computer either manually (static) or automatically (dynamic). This IP address identifies your computer on the network. The IP Address serves a purpose similar to that of home addresses. **Dynamic Host Configuration Protocol (DHCP)** servers assign IP addresses to computers that log on to a particular network. Most computers are assigned IP addresses automatically. When a computer connects with the DHCP server, it receives an IP address that remains in effect for a pre-set period determined by the network administrator. When that time expires, the computer must request another IP address, which it receives automatically from the DHCP server. Although some devices require a permanent IP address that never changes, most servers, particularly those that host your favorite web sites, have IP addresses that do not change. These are called **Static IP addresses**.

FINDING YOUR COMPUTER'S IP ADDRESS

To find your IP address, follow these simple steps. On a PC running Windows go to **Start, Run. In the run box type** *cmd*. (**Start, Programs, MSDOS** on Windows 95, 98 and ME). From there you will be routed to the **Command Prompt (DOS),** you will see a window with a black background showing **C:\>** or similar, depending on your operating system, type in **ipconfig (or winipcfg for Windows 95 and 98).** You will then be given your IP address.

Mac User (OS 9)

Go to **the Apple icon**, then the **Control Panel**, then to **TCP/IP**, and look for your IP address.

Mac User (OS X)

Go to **the Apple icon**. Scroll to **System Preferences**. In the **Internet & Network** category, double-click the **Network** icon. Choose the **TCP/IP** tab, and record your IP address.

NETWORK/ETHERNET CABLING AND EQUIPMENT

Ethernet is the most popular physical network architecture ever conceived. It began in the 1960s at the University of Hawaii as the ALOHA network. On a network, computers must send signals to communicate. **Ethernet cables** tie computers together into networks. Most computers have what is called a **Network Interface Card (NIC)** that allows you to plug in the Ethernet cable and connect to a network. Most NIC cards come in 10/100 speeds. The newer cards come in 10/100/1000 speeds.

Types of Ethernet Cables: Although they look like phone cables, Ethernet cables, also called **CAT 5 UTP**, have a bigger connector and are capable of transmitting more data at a faster speed. Phone lines and Ethernet lines are different and incompatible.

- **Patch Cable** is used to connect the NIC on your computer with a hub, switch or directly into the wall.

- **Crossover cable** is used either to connect two computers together without a hub or switch, or to uplink one hub to another when an uplink port is not available or to a daisy chain on a network device like a Cable modem. **This cable is commonly used to transfer data or communicate directly with another computer**.

- **CAT 1 cable** is the lowest grade networking cable used for Alarm systems and intercom systems; it has no frequency and a speed of 1Mbps.

- **CAT 2 cable** is used typically for phone systems with a 1mhz frequency and a speed of 4Mbps.

- **CAT 3 cable** is a typical low grade10base-T network cable with a frequency of 16MHz and a speed of 10Mbps.

- **CAT 4 cable** is mostly used on token ring networks with a frequency of 20MHz and a speed of 16Mbps.

- **CAT 5 cable** is the most common type of cable used in 10Mbps and 100Mbps networks with a frequency of 100MHz and a speed of 100Mbps.

- **CAT 5e and CAT 6 cable** are the newest high-speed cable used in Gigabit networks with a frequency of approximately 350MHz and a speed of 1,000Mbps.
- **CAT 7 cable** is currently under development.

It is acceptable to use a faster, higher grade cable than needed as this will leave room for future network upgrades.

HUBS, SWITCHES, AND ROUTERS

Everything sent through Ethernet networks is cut into small bits of data known as **packets**. The computer sending the information gives the packets an address and sends them down the cable. A **hub** and a **switch** enable you to connect many computers or printers from one Ethernet port.

If the packet comes to a **hub**, the hub copies the packet and sends it to every other port. Thus, in a 4-port hub with three computers attached, each computer connected to the hub will receive the packet. Once the packet gets to the proper destination, the intended computer sees its address on the packet and accepts it. With a hub, if computers or printers try to send information on the line at the same time, a data collision occurs and the packets must be re-submitted. As you can see, a hub would not be a good choice when dealing with heavy data transmissions.

A switch learns the addresses of the individual systems beforehand. When a packet of data comes to it, the switch looks at the address and sends the packet to its proper destination without sending it to the other ports. This is why a switch is preferable to a hub when there is heavy network traffic.

Routers are specifically designed to connect two networks such as a **LAN (Local Area Network)** and a **WAN (Wide Area Network).** A router has built-in **firewall** software with security features that prohibit unauthorized access to the computers from outside. Also, home users or users with DSL or Cable modems may be assigned only one IP address to access the Internet. To connect another computer to the Internet, technically (and LEGALLY), you would need another IP address from the Cable or DSL company. There is, however, a router technology called **Network Address Translation (NAT)**, that splits or translates, the single IP address into up to 253 different private IP addresses. Each computer connected to the router can then access the Internet individually.

9

Wireless Networking

Wireless computing is the ability to connect to the Internet, access file servers and printers, and send and receive e-mail without wires (i.e., through Ethernet cables). Wireless computing has two main components: an **access point** and a **wireless PC Card**. The access point converts the Ethernet connection into radio waves. The wireless PC card communicates with the access point that enables the desktop or laptop to connect to the Internet wirelessly.

WIRELESS STANDARDS...802.11

Wireless standards come in different flavors to address the varied speeds, interoperability, and ranges. The standards presently in place include the **802.11b**, the **802.11a**, and the **802.11g**. Although theses standards all address the wireless spectrum, they cannot always be intermingled due to incompatibility issues. The most widely used standard is currently 802.11b, it is rapidly being replaced by the 802.11g.

When considering wireless, most products and organizations focus on the 802.11b and g standards.

Wireless Standard	Max. Speed	Approximate Range	Frequency	Features
802.11b	11Mbps	150ft. indoors 2,000ft. Outdoors	2.4GHz	Supported by many products and most widely used Could experience interference
802.11a	54Mbps	60ft. indoors 1,600ft outdoors	5GHz	Supported by fewer products. Fast speeds with less short range interference
802.11g	54Mbps	60ft. indoors 1,600ft. outdoors	5GHz and 2.4GHz	Fast speeds with backward compatibility

WIRELESS SECURITY

Security is a big issue when implementing a wireless strategy. As long as there is a wireless device emitting wireless signals, anyone within range with a wireless-capable computer can use the resource. Ways to address this problem include **encryption** and **authentication**, including **Wireless Equivalent Privacy (WEP)**. Encryption is the process of converting data into a secret form. The minimum acceptable encryption standard is between 64-bit and 128-bit, with the latter being preferred. Standards within this range are more difficult to decode. The WEP encryption method can create a false sense of security, as there are well-known security holes that allow easy exploitation of this method. A form of authentication security that ensures only authorized users can gain access to a resource is called a **Virtual Private Network (VPN),** is by far the best strategy for wireless security.

Authentication is a wireless security technology that verifies a person's identity using a login name and password as with a VPN or by registering the unique address of each network card of a computer.

Wireless Security Method	Advantages	Disadvantages
Encryption	Makes Data difficult to decode by unauthorized individuals	Can be easily compromised and broken into
Authentication	Requires a unique I.D and password	Can be compromised with various equipment
Use a Single Wireless Brand Name	Keeps all units on the same security level making administering easier	May cause incompatibility with different equipment that may be added later

(Wireless Security continued)

Wireless Security Method	Advantages	Disadvantages
Keep Wireless Signal (BaseStation) Confined Indoors	The wireless signal stays within the confines of the building and not intercepted from outside	Could cause signal degradation and poorer ranges allowing fewer individuals to connect within the building
Use VPN Software	Very difficult to break into due to the extra level of security. By far best security method	Can cause various connectivity problems

802.11i

802.11i is a wireless technology that will incorporate stronger encryption techniques, such as **Advanced Encryption Standard (AES)**. An issue, however, is that AES requires a co-processor (additional hardware) to operate. This means that companies need to replace existing access points and client NICs to implement AES. Based on marketing reports, the installed base today is relatively small compared to future deployments. As a result, a large percentage of new wireless LAN implementations will take advantage of AES when it becomes part of the 802.11 standard. Companies that have installed wireless LANs will need to determine whether it is worth the cost to upgrade for better security.

WIRELESS INTERFERENCE

There are many external devices that can degrade or interfere with the wireless signal. These devices include:

- **Microwave Ovens:** Try not to locate your base station near a microwave.
- **2.4GHz cordless phones:** These higher range phones can interfere with wireless reception. As a result, you may want to consider 900MHz cordless phones or wired phones if you experience problems.
- **Concrete walls:** Concrete walls, or other very thick walls, can reduce the range of wireless signals. Specialized antennas or extra access points (base stations) may be required in environments where this is a problem.
- **Buildings and exterior walls:** Wireless signals can go through thin walls, windows and other objects, but for security, make sure the access points are placed so the signal does not travel beyond windows and outside walls. If the signal does go beyond these barriers, make sure it degrades enough so that unauthorized access is prevented.

WIRELESS DEVICES

- **Wireless Gateway** is ideal for a home or small office.
- **Wireless Access Point** is ideal for larger offices and supports encryption.
- **Wireless Enterprise Access Point** is ideal for a wireless enterprise with many users. It supports 10/100Mbps speeds and features high security protection.
- The **Wireless PC Card** provides wireless access for your notebook (laptop).
- The **Wireless PCI Adapter** provides wireless access for your desktop.

- The **Wireless USB** provides wireless access for small form factor computers where PCI adapters cannot be installed.
- The **Wireless Pocket Device Adapter** provides wireless access for pocket devices.

WIRELESS MANUFACTURERS

Overall, products from different wireless vendors are compatible and can function with relatively few problems. Yet some manufacturers offer additional features (such as computer operating system compatibility or advanced security options) that are not compatible with other manufacturers' products. Thus, it is best to stick to one vendor to maximize the wireless configuration options and keep compatibility and security at a premium. Some of the main wireless companies are:

- Cisco Systems
- 3COM
- Intel
- Orinoco
- Linksys
- NetGear
- Apple

In spite of advertising claims, all wireless cards and base stations do not function in the same way. Some cards may not perform as well with respect to signal reception, security, and speed. Be sure to purchase a card that offers firmware upgrades to keep up with the changes in the wireless industry. Before purchasing wireless equipment for an office system, check with your IT Staff about compatibility issues. For home wireless networking, do your homework.

WIRELESS FINDER

There are many web sites available outlining functioning wireless signals that are accessible throughout the world. Some of the wireless points are free to access and some require a fee. The following links list various web sites showing the wireless signals to which you can connect either free of charge or for a fee. Look for signals in your area. **NOTE: You must be physically near the signal in order to connect.**

1. http://www.wifinder.com/
2. http://www.nodedb.com/
3. http://www.toaster.net/wireless/community.html
4. http://www.apdirectory.com/

BLUETOOTH WIRELESS

Bluetooth enables short-range wireless connections by using radio waves between desktop and laptop computers; palm pilot devices, mobile phones, camera phones, printers, digital cameras, and computer keyboard and mouse products. To communicate using the Bluetooth technology, however, all devices must have a built-in Bluetooth communication card.

PART IV

E-Mail, Interfaces, and Connectivity

10

E-Mail

E-MAIL PROGRAMS

To send and receive e-mail, users have a variety of programs from which to choose. Each of these programs has different features that the user may find appealing.

	Outlook	Outlook 2001-Mac	Outlook Express	Eudora
Platform	PC	Macintosh	PC and Macintosh	PC and Macintosh
When Mail Is Received	Remains on the Mail Server Can also Have Mail Downloaded to Hard Drive	Remains on the Mail Server	Downloaded to Your Hard Drive Can Also Have Mail Saved on Mail Server	Downloaded to Your Hard Drive Can Also Have Mail Saved on Mail Server
Advantages	Easy Integration Within Corporate Structure Has Many Customizable Options and Features Compatible With Palm Pilot	Easy Integration Within Corporate Structure Is Directly Compatible With the PC version of Outlook Password Protected	Easy to Learn and Use Easy to Import/Export Mail from Other E-mail Programs Compatible With Palm Pilot	Downloads Attachments to A Separate Folder on the Hard Drive Can Read Old Mail and Compose Mail While Not Connected to Network
Disadvantages	Main Target of Virus Writers	Has no POP3 Option Is not Compatible With Palm Pilot	Has Few Customizable or Powerful Features	Has Few Customizable or Powerful Features

(E-mail Programs Continued)

	Netscape Mail	Entourage	PINE
Platform	PC, Linux and Macintosh	Macintosh	PC, Linux and Macintosh
When Mail Is Received	Downloaded to Your Hard Drive Can Also Have Mail Saved on Mail Server	Downloaded to Your Hard Drive Can Also Have Mail Saved on Mail Server	Remains on the mail server
Advantages	Easy to Learn and Use Can Read Old Mail and Compose Mail While Not Connected to Network	Easy to Learn and Use Compatible With Palm Pilot Can Read Old Mail and Compose Mail While Not Connected to Network	Easy to Learn and Use Commonly used by Universities
Disadvantages	Has Few Customizable or Powerful Features	Works with Macintosh Computers Only Has Few Customizable or Powerful Features	Password can Easily be Obtained by Hackers Has No Customizable Features

How E-Mail is Accessed and Stored

The process of retrieving e-mail works like a P.O. box. When mail is received from a sender, it first goes to the mail server where it waits for you to pick it up, thus removing it from the mail server's box to your own box. In the case of e-mail, the message is downloaded to your hard drive and you can adjust the e-mail program to save a copy of the message on the server for a specified number of days. Thus, if you were to use an Internet-based e-mail viewer such as www.mail2web.com to view your mail, you would be able to view the newly received mail as well as your old e-mail messages.

Many companies use a Microsoft mail component called **Exchange** that keeps all of the mail and contacts on an Exchange Server. The mail remains on the Exchange Server until the user removes it by archiving or deleting the mail from their Inbox. Fortunately, when using Exchange, the network administrator can set rules to prevent individuals from abusing their e-mail privileges. Mail programs that integrate best with Microsoft Exchange include Microsoft Outlook and Microsoft Outlook for Macintosh.

When setting up an e-mail program, two important names to know are the **SMTP** server and the **POP3** server. The Exchange Server is important for setting up e-mail via Exchange. Check with your local **Internet Service Provider (ISP)** or the network administrator in your office to determine the mail server settings if you plan to use one of the many e-mail programs.

11

Computer Viruses and Worms

A computer **virus** is a program that can reproduce itself and spread from one file to another on a **single computer**. A computer **worm** is a program designed to copy itself from **one computer to another** usually by way of a network, e-mail, or any resource that is shared by many users. The main objective of the computer worm is to infect as many machines as possible on a shared network. A **Trojan horse** is a program that infects a computer and is capable of changing file settings, stealing passwords, destroying files or installing illegal programs.

WHO MAKES COMPUTER VIRUSES

Computer viruses are human-made programming code produced by someone with a basic knowledge of computer programming. They can be, and have been, written by anyone, anywhere in the world. With more than 90 percent of the world's desktop computers running Windows (PC) platforms, small wonder that more than 99 percent of all computer viruses were/are designed to exploit that environment. In addition, the Windows platform is well documented, easily programmable, and full of erroneous programming code.

HOW VIRUSES SPREAD

Viruses are usually spread by the computer user. Downloading programs from the Internet, sharing diskettes, opening e-mail attachments, or file sharing within a network can spread them. So, computer viruses are acquired through any form of data sharing via a network or removable disks.

TYPES OF VIRUSES

There are many different viruses designed to attack computers and networks. Although worms, viruses, and Trojan horses are technically different, for these purposes I will categorize all as viruses. Some of the more common viruses include:

- **E-mail Worms**

  This virus uses e-mail as the primary mode of transportation. It spreads by leveraging the address book of each person who unknowingly executes (i.e., releases) the virus by opening the accompanying attachment. These worms pose a major threat to corporate mail servers by clogging them with a constantly repeated message. Simply reading an e-mail that has a virus, however, cannot release the virus. The virus can only be released when the user actually opens the attachment. Hence, these viruses are sometimes called **user-launched worms**. Increasingly, however, virus writers are looking for ways to release a virus as soon as the user reads the message. These **self-launching** worms will be a major concern in years to come.

- **Macro viruses**

  A **macro** is a collection of instructions to be carried out by a program. Macros are not intended to be harmful to computer systems, but are designed to make computing faster and easier for the user, particularly with Microsoft Word or Excel. Macros usually handle repetitive tasks. For example, instead of having to add your name, address, phone number, date of birth, and other information into many documents, the macro automates the process for you with the press of a button. Macros can be designed to perform this task with any data that involves repetition. A macro virus is created by someone who wishes to exploit the utility of the macro. The macro virus can infect both PC and Macintosh computers. Once the computer is infected, any Word or Excel document that is created or opened may also contain the virus. Keep in mind that a **virus designed for a Macintosh cannot spread to a PC and vice versa. Both platforms can only be infected when a virus is designed to infect an entire program, such as Microsoft Word, PowerPoint, and Excel.**

- **Boot Sector Viruses**

  Boot Sector Viruses are spread through the sharing of floppy disks. Any type of diskette (not to be confused with a CD) can spread this virus, which is designed to infect the boot sector of the diskette. The boot sector contains specific instructions and information relating to the formatting (erasing) of a disk, the data stored on the disk, and the boot (start up) program. This is what allows some users to start up their computer from a floppy disk (i.e., to boot from floppy). When the boot sector of a diskette is infected, the virus loads itself into the computer memory and infects the hard drive because a hard drive has a boot sector as well.

- **Trojan Horses**

  Trojan Horses are often programs that install themselves entirely without the user's knowledge. These programs fool the user into believing that they are performing a useful task, when in fact they are designed to steal your identification and passwords. They can then scramble or erase the contents of your hard drive, use your computer to send multiple requests to overload servers, use your computer as a remote server to store illegal software, shut down your computer every Monday at 2 p.m., or display obscene messages. Users who get Trojan Horses are picked up when the user unknowingly downloads a program that promises something useful or interesting. Trojan Horses, however, do not spread like viruses. They typically infect the computer that runs the program. Yet it will remain on that computer until the program is removed manually or automatically by anti-virus software.

- **Program Viruses**

  Sharing programs spreads Program Viruses. A program virus can also infect other programs on a computer and damage important files needed by the program to run properly. Luckily, most users do not share programs as frequently making this type of virus less common.

- **E-mail Hoax**

  This is not a virus. It is a rumor of a hideous virus that will erase your hard drive or some other imaginary story of computer data doom. It usually starts with a person creating a **false e-mail** message instructing everyone to look out for a virus or to delete a file on their computer and to send a copy of the e-mail to family and friends.

VIRUS SYMPTOMS

Different viruses cause different symptoms. Some common virus-related computer problems may include:

- Slower computer operation

- Unusual disk activity (constant disk spinning noise)

- A sudden and significant decrease in hard drive space

- Constant system crashes

- The display of annoying and/or obscene dialogue box messages

- Un-requested animations on the computer screen

- The sudden appearance of programs, files or folders that you did not install or create

- Multiple e-mails from the same person, or different persons, with the same subject and the same message

HOW TO AVOID VIRUSES

One of the best ways to avoid viruses is to install anti-virus software in your computer. Use software from companies like Symantec, F-Secure, Kaspersky, McAfee, Trend Micro and Central Command and regularly download the latest anti-virus updates that become available. These companies employ computer programmers whose job is to find ways to stop viruses by creating anti-virus computer code, known as **anti-virus definitions** or **anti-virus updates**. They spend all day testing computer code and looking for viruses as more viruses are created, which is why anti-virus definitions are regularly updated.

Other ways to avoid viruses include:

• Scan floppy disks and zip disks you intend to use, especially if you use a disk given to you by someone else. Also, scan diskettes and zip disks after using them on a computer other than your own. Scan your computer after installing data from a burned CD or DVD.

• Create a strong password incorporating letters, numbers and symbols.

• Disable accounts on your computer without passwords.

• If you receive an e-mail message from someone whom you do not know and it contains an attachment, delete it.

• Scan attachments you receive from people you know, as those attachments could be infected.

• Scan files you download from the Internet.

• Scan compressed files and zip files. Also scan files and programs received from FTP sites.

• Enable your anti-virus software to run in the background throughout the day.

REMOVING VIRUSES

What to do if you have a virus, or think you have a virus

If your computer is behaving strangely and you think you have a virus, make sure you have the most current anti-virus update and run a full computer virus scan. Keep in mind, however, that not all damage or erratic computer activity is caused by a virus. A bad floppy disk, zip disk, or bad CD can cause your computer to crash or freeze. A failing hard drive can cause your computer to crash or exhibit unusual noises. In addition, new software and hardware (printers, camcorders, CD-Burners, etc.) can cause your computer to behave in a strange manner. Indeed, the anti-virus software used to protect your computer can also cause the computer to behave strangely, run more slowly than normal, or crash. If your computer does have a virus, don't panic. Here are some steps you can take.

- Update the anti-virus definitions on your computer and run a full scan of your hard drive or go to Symantec or Sophos web site to obtain the removal tools and manual removal instructions.

- If you happen to open an e-mail attachment that contains a virus, shut down the e-mail program and run a full computer virus scan or obtain the removal tool as above.

- If you received a hoax e-mail and, as a result, deleted a file, there is probably a fix available on the web site of the company that manufactured your anti-virus software.

THE FUTURE OF SPREADING VIRUSES

Cable/DSL Connected Users and Home Networks

With the increase in home users switching to faster modes of Internet access and networking home computers, printers and scanners, attacks by malicious viruses will become a more common occurrence. Those who keep their computer connected all day and all night will be especially vulnerable to attack. As a result, firewall and anti-virus protection will be an absolute necessity.

Mutating Worms

These viruses will be capable of changing and reproducing different sequences of instructions for themselves, thus rendering them more difficult to catch and delete.

Stubborn Worms

These viruses will attempt to render themselves almost impossible to remove from a system.

Wireless Worms

With so many wireless devices capable of sending and receiving a host of information (e-mail, voice, photos, etc.), virus writers will surely target such devices. If such a worm takes form, it will have a devastating effect on the wireless industry, given our increasing reliance on this form of communication.

12

Spam

Unsolicited commercial e-mail, more commonly known as **spam**, is junk e-mail sent to your inbox by individuals and businesses (i.e., spammers) unknown to you.

HOW DO SPAMMERS FIND YOU

Spammers find their victims in numerous ways. The techniques include, but are by no means limited to, newsgroups, chat rooms, Web sites, AOL user profile lists, Internet white and yellow pages, mail list servers, chain-letter hoaxes that trick you into replying, software packages that make up thousands of e-mail addresses, then send them out blindly and track addresses that did not bounce back, and former online companies that went out of business and sold their mailing lists.

WAYS TO AVOID SPAM

There is no way to get rid of all spam. The risk when an anti-spam campaign is in place is that legitimate e-mail can be destroyed, especially when using third-party anti-spam software. Here are some simple methods you can use to minimize the amount of spam you receive.

- Do not reply to a spam e-mail or use a link that the spammer claims will remove you from their mailing list. In many cases this just lets the spammer know you're alive. Keep in mind that legitimate companies will actually remove you from a list if you so request.

- Only use your work e-mail address for work-related communication with legitimate companies. Remember also that you can refuse to give your e-mail address to a requesting company if asked.

- If you receive the same category of spam, such as pornography or business opportunities, or if the sender is the same, you should use the e-mail filtering utility of your e-mail program to set filters. Keep in mind, however, that some legitimate e-mail may be filtered. Do not set the filter to automatically delete e-mails, rather set the filter to send them to a spam folder for later viewing.

- Sign up for a free Hotmail or Yahoo e-mail account and if an e-mail address is needed for some service, give that address instead of your work.

- Earthlink.net does a pretty good job at stopping spam from entering users inboxes. Yahoo mail, and AOL also have good built-in anti-spam features.

THE FUTURE OF SPAM

The federal **CAN-SPAM Act** is supposed to punish bulk e-mailers by requiring them to include their valid return address and making it illegal to obtain addresses from web sites, e-mail servers, or e-mail address generating programs. This is only one of many laws that will probably be passed to combat spam. In the end, however, only honest companies are likely to abide by the laws. Companies that operate outside the United States and outside the law will continue their spam assault. So keep up your spam guards.

PART V
Data Saved

13

Data Back up

All information you keep on your computer is stored on your hard drive. Since hard drives have parts moving at very fast speeds, the possibility of a failure at some point is great. There is also the possibility of a fire, flood, or theft. Because of this, it is always beneficial to keep backups of your important information. **Backing up** your data involves copying the data to an alternate location, whether that is on a floppy disk, making a copy to a CD-R/RW or DVD (burning to a disk), or saving it to data tapes.

I. INFORMATION TO BACK UP

- Important irreplaceable data

- Important correspondence

- Internal documents (important memos and letters)

- Anything that would cause your work to become difficult if the data were lost

- Works in progress, drafts, sensitive data, databases, unique JPEG, TIFF and GIFF images and data, breakthrough discoveries

- Important e-mails, contacts, web site bookmarks and music

- Business-critical information

II. INFORMATION NOT NEEDING BACK UP

- Your computer's operating system

- Software from the computer (Since most software copied from a PC will not always function properly. However, Macintosh has better success)

- Data easily retrieved from other sources
- Temp files
- Anything that would not cause your work to become difficult if lost

III. How Often Should You Back up Your Data

- Ask yourself how many days worth of information could you afford to lose if your computer crashed
- How often do you access particular data from day-to-day?
- Major works in progress should be backed up on a daily basis or right after changes are made
- Information that can cause hardship to complete your daily work duties should be backed up on a daily basis
- Data that would not cause hardship can be backed up on a weekly or monthly basis, depending on the level of importance

IV. How to and Where to Back up Data

- **Direct CD**. For Daily backups one of the best solutions is to use **Adaptec Direct CD**, with this program you use a CD-R or CD-RW as the back up medium. Simply start the Direct CD wizard, insert the blank disk, allow Direct CD to format the disk and simply drag and drop what you would like to copy to the CD.
- **Transportable External Hard Drive**. Many companies including Iomega, LaCie and Smart-Disk have devices that allow you to back up and store your data in a small portable casing. These devices are easy to use and can be used on different computers by plugging in a USB cable or FireWire Cable.
- **Burning Data to a CD-R or DVD-R/DVD+R**. For the monthly back up regimen, burning the data to a CD-R or DVD-R/DVD+R is a good option.

Options When Hard Drives Go Bad Containing Important Data

People who save their important data exclusively on their computer hard drives are only asking for trouble. Sometimes hard drives can crash to the point where it no longer spins. When this happens your hard drive will not allow you to access your data, basically, your hard drive is dead, like a dead light bulb. In short, there is nothing that you or your computer support department can do. Even if you have insurance from the computer manufacturer they will not be able to help you with the retrieval of your data or even pay for the retrieval process. They will, however, send and install a new hard drive.

Luckily, there are companies specializing in this type of scenario. A company called **Drive Savers** is one of them. How much you pay for the data retrieval will depend on the size of the hard drive and the severity of the damage. Prices usually range from $500 to $3,000, it's a steep price but if you did not employ a backup strategy and very important data is needed from the hard drive, this is your only recourse. **Keep in mind that retrieving lost data may not always be successful**. Back Up or Pay Up!

14

Optical Storage

The new revolution in storage is in the form of CDs. Gone are the days of the floppy disk and soon the zip disk will make way for the CD and the fast approaching DVD.

Burning a CD is the new technology allowing the storage of data and music. A CD-Recorder (also called CD-R drive, CD-ReadWrite, CD-Burner or CD-Writer) can record to two different types of blank CD Media, namely CD-R and CD-RW. To maximize the speed of your CD Burner, make sure you buy blank disks that meet or exceed the speed of the burner. If your burner is a 32x burner buy disks that are 32x speed.

When you **burn** a CD you are actually burning dyes and creating phase changes. All recordable CDs use one of two kinds of dye and it is the dye that is burned by the CD recorder's laser beam that creates pits. During playback these pits are read by another laser beam. CD-RW, however, does not actually burn pits in the disc but changes the structure of the crystals and metals found in the disk. Either way, the disk is heated and a phase change takes place within the disk.

WHAT DO THE NUMBERS MEAN?

A CD Burner's performance is measured by its speed. For example, a burner will be advertised with a speed of 12x 10x 40x. These numbers represent the how fast the burner burns data if it were recording to a CD-R disk, a CD-RW disk and a how fast a CD with data is read. In our example, 12x corresponds to the burning of a CD-R disk, 10x corresponds to the burning of a CD-RW disk and 40x is the speed at which a disk is read. So, we can say (**12x10x40x = CD-R, CD-RW, CD-ROM**). Higher numbers usually equate to a faster burner. Make sure the blank CDs that you buy matches the speed of your burner or else you will not achieve the highest possible speeds.

CD-R

This particular disk is the most popular and can be used once only, yet most of the CD-Recording software today including Adaptec Easy CD Creator, Toast, and Nero allow users to add to the disk in more than one recording session until it's full. This is called **multi-session recording**. For example, you can record some files and then go back and record more files at a later time.

CD-RW

Blank CD-RW media make it possible to record thousands of times to the same disk. This is a good choice for short-term data. Recording to this media, however, is slower than the CD-R media due to the phase-change that has to take place to allow recording over previously recorded data.

DVD-RAM

DVD-RAM is a re-writable media that can be written and re-written more than 100,000 times. The disk comes enclosed in a cartridge. It offers some of the biggest storage capacities allowing up to 9.4GB of data. DVD-RAM discs come in a **Type 1 Cartridge,** which does not allow removal of the disc, and a **Type 2 Cartridge**, which allows the removal of the disc.

DVD+RW

This re-writable media was developed and proposed by Hewlett-Packard, Philips, and Sony with collaboration with Verbatim, Ricoh and Yamaha. The main purpose of this media is to allow compatibility with existing DVD-ROM drives and do away with the need for a cartridge like in DVD-RAM. These discs are usually not compatible with DVD-RW drives.

DVD-RW

This media allows temporary storage of data or information that is regularly updated. A single disc can be recorded up to 1,000 times. These discs are usually not compatible with DVD+RW drives.

DVD-R

Once data is burned to this media it is permanent and cannot be changed or altered. If you plan to burn movies, DVD-R tends to perform better in home DVD players.

DVD+R

This media uses similar technology as the DVD+RW, however, it can be copied to only once and it does not utilize a cartridge. This media also claims to support faster burning speeds.

DVD-R (AUTHORING)

This is a copy-once media that uses material that enhances the characteristics for reliable video, imaging and graphics. Other non-multimedia data can be written to this sort of disc as well. The price of this media tends to be more expensive, however.

Chart of CD MEDIA

	CD-ROM Compact Disk – Read Only Memory	CD-RW Compact Disk – ReWritable	CD-R Compact Disk – Recordable
Purpose	Stores Large Amounts of Data including Music	Storage of Data Determined by The User	Storage of Data Determined by The User
Data Storage Capacity	Up to 680MB per disc	650 – 700MB of Data Up to 80 Minutes of Music	650 – 700MB of Data Up to 80 Minutes of Music
Speed	Speed is based on the CD-ROM Drive Used	1X – 10X	1X – 40X and Increasing
Advantages	Can store a variety of Data including Music Disc Can be Copied	Data can be Copied and Erased over a Thousand Times	Records Data at A Relatively Fast Pace Are Compatible With Most CD Players
Disadvantages	Disc comes with data pre-written and cannot be written over	The Recording Process is Relatively Slow Are Incompatible with Some Older CD Players	Data Cannot be Erased Once Written
Multi-Session Recording	NO	YES	YES

Chart of DVD MEDIA

	DVD-ROM Digital Versatile (Video) Disc	DVD-RAM Digital Versatile Disc – Random Access Memory	DVD-RW Digital Versatile Disc – ReWritable	DVD+RW Digital Versatile Disc Plus ReWritable
Purpose	Very Large Storage of Data including Movies	Very Large Storage of Data including Movies	Very Large Storage of Data including Movies	Very Large Storage of Data including Movies
Data Storage Capacity Speed	4.7GB – 17 GB 200 – 500 RPM	4.7GB– 17 GB 1X – 4X	4.7GB – 17GB 1X – 4X	4.7GB – 17GB 1X – 4X
Advantages	Stores Far More Data Than CD-ROM	Data Can be Copied and Erased Many Thousands of Times	Data Can be Copied and Erased Many Thousands of Times Can burn CD-R/RW Discs	Data Can be Copied Many Thousands of Times Can burn CD-R/RW Discs
Disadvantages	Cannot Record Data	Uses a Cartridge Cannot be Used in a CD-ROM Drive DVD Player Compatibility Issues	Not Compatible With all DVD Players Cannot Be Used in A CD-Rom Drive	Not Compatible With all DVD Players Cannot be Used in A CD-ROM Drive
Multi-Session Recording	NO	Varies	Varies	Varies

(DVD MEDIA Continued)

	DVD-R/+R **Digital Versatile Disc – Recordable**	DVD-R **(Authoring)** **Digital Versatile Disc Plus Recordable**
Purpose	Very Large Storage of Data including Movies	Very Large Storage of Data Specifically Multi-media
Data Storage Capacity	4.7GB – 17GB	4.7GB
Speed	1X – 4X	1X – 4X
Advantages	Can Copy Data	Can improve the recording and playback of multimedia
Disadvantages	Not Compatible With all DVD Players Cannot be Used in a CD-ROM Drive	Not Compatible With all DVD Players Media tends to be more Expensive Cannot be Used in a CD-ROM Drive
Multi-Session Recording	Varies	Varies

15

Hardware Interfaces

When a device—whether printer, CD-Burner, hard drive, floppy drive, zip drive, scanner, etc.—is connected to a computer, it must have the proper matching **interface** to communicate with the computer. An interface is the port having the wires, plugs and sockets that devices use to communicate with each other and the computer.

There are many interfaces to choose from all offering different performance, speed and cost. Most computers, including laptops, are shipped with a number of different interfaces already installed—usually serial, parallel, USB, and IDE.

When choosing a new device to connect to your computer, the type of interface you intend to connect it to can be an important decision. If speed, convenience and mobility are concerns then **FireWire** (also called **IEEE 1394**) would be a top choice. **USB 2.0** is another good candidate for this purpose. Keep in mind, however, when purchasing these interfaces that many older computers do not support them, in which case you will have to purchase a FireWire Card, in the case of FireWire. With regard to USB 2.0 many computers, even some of newer models, do not support the faster data transfer rate. Although the device would work with the existing USB port, the faster USB 2.0 speed would not be achieved—that's where a USB 2.0 card would help. In addition, Windows NT does not support USB. Other interface descriptions include:

SERIAL

Set up is easy yet the data transfer can be slow. Also, this is an older technology that many of the newer devices may not support.

PARALLEL

Also called **IEEE 1294**, set up is easy yet the data transfer can be slow. This is an older technology that many of the newer devices may not support. Printers commonly use this interface.

USB

Set up is very easy and the performance is generally good yet not for devices requiring faster speeds. Not compatible with Windows NT.

USB 2.0

Set up is easy and performance is very good. It has a very fast speed yet many computers, including some of the newer models, do not support the speed without having to buy a USB 2.0 adapter card. Not compatible with Windows NT.

FireWire (IEEE 1394)

Developed by Apple Computer Corporation. Also called **IEEE 1394** by the PC community, set up is easy and the performance is considered to be excellent. Can be costly. Although it is standard equipment on most Macintosh computers, it is not included on most PCs, yet a FireWire adapter card could be purchased.

	Serial	Parallel	USB 1.1
Maximum Transfer Rate	.01MBps	.15MBps	1.5MBps – 12MBps
Maximum Connections	1 device	1 device	127 devices
Cable Connector	9-pin	25-pin	Slot Loaded
Advantages	Easy to Connect Devices	Easy to Connect Devices	Very Easy to Connect Devices Can Plug and Unplug While Computer and Device are Running
Disadvantages	Slow, Older Technology	Slow, Older Technology	Slower Data Transfer Speed Does not Work on Windows NT

(Interface Continued)

	USB 2.0	FireWire (IEEE 1394)	FireWire b (IEEE 1394b)	FireWire c (IEEE 1394c)
Maximum Transfer Rate	480MBps	400MBps	800MBps	Over 900MBps
Maximum Connections	127 devices	62 devices	62 devices	62 devices
Cable Connector	Slot-Style Plug	Plug	Plug	Plug
Advantages	Very Easy to Connect Devices

Can Plug and Unplug While Computer and Device are Running | Very Easy to Connect Devices

Can Plug and Unplug While Computer and Device are Running | Plug and Unplug While Computer and Device are Running | Very Easy to Connect Devices

Can Plug and Unplug While Computer and Device are Running |
| Disadvantages | Not Included on Older Computer Systems

Does not Work on Windows NT | Can be Expensive

Not Included on Older Computer Systems | Can be Expensive

Not included on Older Computer Systems | Newest FireWire not yet implemented |

IDE

This interface comes in different flavors and goes by many different names including: **ATA, EIDE, Ultra ATA, ATAPI**, and the newest interfaces in the ATA lineup called **SATA** or **Serial ATA**. Set up is moderately difficult since the computer must be opened and proper cables must be used. This is the main interface that connects most computer hard drives. The performance is relatively good and faster than serial, parallel and USB.

	IDE (ATA)	EIDE (ATA-2)	EIDE (ATA-3)	Ultra ATA/33	Ultra ATA/66
Maximum Data Transfer Rate	3.3 – 8MBps	11-16MBps	16MBps	33MBps	66MBps
Maximum Connections	2	2	2	2 per cable	2 per cable
Cable Connector	40-pin	40-pin	40-pin	40-pin	40-pin, 80 conductor
Advantages	Good Performance. Can Connect two Devices on the Same Cable	Good Performance. Can Connect two Devices on the Same Cable	Good Performance. Can Connect two Devices on the Same Cable	Good Performance. Can Connect two Devices on the Same Cable	Good Performance. Can Connect two Devices on the Same Cable
Disadvantages	Must open Computer. Can be difficult to set-up	Must open Computer. Can be difficult to set-up	Must open Computer. Can be difficult to set-up	Must open Computer. Can be difficult to set-up	Must open Computer. Can be difficult to set-up

(IDE INTERFACE Continued)

	Ultra ATA/100	Ultra ATA/133	Serial ATA I	SATA II
Maximum Data Transfer Rate	100MBps	133MBps	150MBps	300MBps
Maximum Connections	2 per cable	2 per cable	15 per port	15 per port
Cable Connector	40-pin, 80 conductor	40-pin, 80 conductor	7-pin	7-pin
Advantages	Good Performance. Can Connect two Devices on the Same Cable	Good Performance. Can Connect two Devices on the Same Cable	Faster and Simpler Connector	Fast and hot swappable
Disadvantages	Must open Computer. Can be difficult to set-up	Must open Computer. Can be difficult to set-up	Not widely supported	Not widely supported

SCSI

Pronounced (*scuzzy*), set up can be very difficult but the performance and speed is by far the best, especially when multiple devices are used. Each device needs a SCSI card, however.

	SCSI-1	SCSI-2	Ultra-SCSI	Wide Ultra SCSI
Maximum Data Transfer Rate	5MBps	10MBps	20MBps	40MBps
Maximum Connections	8 devices	8 devices	4 – 8 devices	4 – 8 devices
Cable Connector	50-pin	50-pin	50-pin	68-pin
Advantages	Very Fast and Stable Performance	Very Fast and Stable Performance	Very Fast and Stable Performance	Very Fast and Stable Performance
Disadvantages	Special Hardware Requirements needed Set-up is Difficult	Special Hardware Requirements needed Set-up is Difficult	Special Hardware Requirements needed Set-up is Difficult	Special Hardware Requirements needed Set-up is Difficult

(SCSI Continued)

	Ultra-2 SCSI	Wide Ultra-2 SCSI	Ultra-3/Ultra-160 SCSI	Ultra 320 SCSI
Maximum Data Transfer Rate	40MBps	80MBps	160MBps	320MBps
Maximum Connections	8 devices	8 devices	16 devices	16 devices
Cable Connector Advantages	50-pin Very Fast and Stable Performance	68-pin Very Fast and Stable Performance	68-pin Very Fast and Stable Performance	68-pin Very Fast and Stable Performance
Disadvantages	Special Hardware Requirements needed Set-up is Difficult	Special Hardware Requirements needed Set-up is Difficult	Special Hardware Requirements needed Set-up is Difficult	Special Hardware Requirements needed Set-up is Difficult

PART VI
Making Choices

16

Choosing a Printer

Choosing a printer can be an important decision. The first step to make is defining your needs. Do you intend to use the printer for home or office? Do you plan to use the printer to print word documents, numerical spreadsheets, graphics or pictures? Things to consider include monthly printer usage and print quality since they can affect the cost of your printer. **Inkjet printers** and **LaserJet printers** are the two main print technologies available today and each should be investigated to see if your needs would be met. **Direct Photo Printers** are the newest innovation addressing the digital camera revolution.

DIRECT PHOTO PRINTERS

This is the newest breed of printer that allows the user to print directly from a **digital camera memory card** without using a computer. These printers primarily come in the **color inkjet** format. On some models you can preview, enhance and edit photos using the printer's built-in color LCD. Memory Cards that these printers accept depends on the printer, yet most will accept **Compact-Flash Type I** and **II, SmartMedia, Secure Digital, Multi-Media** cards, and **Sony Memory Stick**. Most of these printers support both PC and Macintosh platforms, as well as Hewlett-Packard digital camera direct printing. Since this is a photo printer, the prints can be very high quality. Yet the cost of ink cartridges will come into play if you intend to print a great number of pictures.

	Black and White	**Color**
Advantages	<ul><li>Affordable</li><li>Good for Users Who Print Occasionally</li><li>Can Preview, Edit and Enhance Photos using the built-in LCD</li></ul>	<ul><li>Affordable</li><li>Produces Very High Quality Prints</li><li>Good for Creating Instant Photos</li><li>Can Print Directly From Your Camera Without Using a Computer</li></ul>
Disadvantages	<ul><li>Slow</li><li>Requires Frequent Change of Ink Cartridge</li><li>Prone to Breakdowns</li><li>Less Precise Printing Process</li><li>The Price Paid for Ink Cartridges and Coated Paper can add up over time</li></ul>	<ul><li>Slow</li><li>Requires Frequent Change of Color Cartridges</li><li>Prone to Breakdowns</li><li>Less Precise Printing Process</li><li>The Price Paid for Ink Cartridges and Coated Paper can add up over time</li></ul>

LASERJET PRINTERS

	Black and White	**Color**
Advantages	<ul><li>Good Quality Prints</li><li>Fast</li><li>Reliable</li><li>Great for Documents and Simple Graphics</li><li>Easier Maintenance</li></ul>	<ul><li>Good Quality</li><li>Fast</li><li>Reliable</li><li>Great for Media in Color</li><li>Easier Maintenance</li></ul>
Disadvantages	<ul><li>Can be Expensive to Purchase and Repair</li></ul>	<ul><li>Can be Expensive to Purchase and Repair</li><li>Can Require Special Printing Paper</li><li>Color Cartridges can be Expensive if Printer is Used Frequently</li></ul>

INKJET PRINTERS

	Black and White	Color
Advantages	• Affordable • Good for Users Who Print Occasionally	• Affordable • Produces Very Good Colors • Good for Users Who Print Occasionally
Disadvantages	• Slow • Requires Frequent Change of Ink Cartridge • Prone to Breakdowns • Less Precise Printing Process • The Price Paid for Ink Cartridges and Coated Paper can add up over time	• Slow • Requires Frequent Change of Color Cartridges • Prone to Breakdowns • Less Precise Printing Process • The Price Paid for Ink Cartridges and Coated Paper can add up over time

PRINTER FEATURES

- **Dot Per Inch (dpi)**

This rating measures the sharpness of printed information. Laser printers produce by far the sharpest prints. Inkjets typically claim output resolutions of 1,200dpi or 2,400dpi or more. The printing sharpness of inkjets is not comparable to that of lasers since inkjet printers use a less precise process where tiny splotches of liquid ink are drawn line by line. Generally, when considering inkjet printers, it's best to ignore inkjet dpi claims and compare actual printouts when possible.

- **Pages Per Minute (ppm)**

This rating determines how many pages the printer is capable of printing each minute. Laser printers generally print text pages slightly slower than the claims made by the manufacturer. The ppm used for inkjets is typically when the printer is set to print at low quality using very simple text pages.

- **PostScript Support**

PostScript is a printing programming language that allows you to scale (shrink) text or data on documents that may otherwise not fit on the page. If you intend to print many documents in this style, in particular excel spreadsheets, make sure your printer is PostScript capable. The **PCL** printing language, which is found on the entry-level printers, does not allow the scaling of documents.

- **OS Support**

    When purchasing a printer, a big issue to consider is your operating system (Windows 95, 98, NT, 2000; Mac OS). Some printers may not offer the proper software to run with your system. Make sure you check that everything is compatible.

BRANDS

All printers, especially inkjet printers, have moving parts that could cause problems with frequent use. Even printers made by reputable companies have their share of problems. A good warranty is a good way to help decrease unexpected expenses. Warranties should be considered on the more expensive LaserJet printers, too. Brands such as Epson, Hewlett-Packard, Brother, Dell, Tektronics and Lexmark are the recognized leaders in the printer industry.

17

Choosing a Scanner

Once you are ready to purchase a scanner, try to determine its intended purpose. If you intend to use the scanner primarily for scanning documents, a simple entry-level model will suffice. Yet if you intend to scan finished photos, negatives, and slides, you should look for a higher quality scanner. Additionally, many scanners also come with optical character recognition, or **OCR**, software that allows you to scan a printed document and convert it to text that can be edited on your PC.

SCANNING CONSIDERATIONS

- **Web Images**

  To scan images for the Web, you only need a scanner that scans photos or slides at 72 ppi. That's because all Web browsers display images at 72 ppi, no matter what resolution they were scanned.

- **Scanning Photos, Negatives and Slides**

  For use in printed material, such as newsletters or greeting cards, you'll want to scan photos at a minimum of 300 ppi–1200 ppi if you can afford it—to get the best possible image quality of your printed material. To reprint color photos, you will want a high-quality photo printer and a high-resolution scanner with at least 24-bit color depth.

- **Scanning Documents and Printed Material**

  If you only plan to scan text documents, you can save a bit of money by choosing a lower resolution (600 ppi) scanner with 16-bit or 24-bit color.

TYPES OF SCANNERS

- **Flatbed Scanners** are the best overall model of scanner especially when books and other bulky items will be scanned.

- **Sheet-fed Scanners** are not as popular due to their lack of versatility. They only allow individual text documents to be scanned; other media may be bent or wrinkled during the feeding process.

- **Handheld Scanners** are used to scan lines of text. They are best used for scanning short citations. This scanner is also called a **pen scanner** and is the newest form of scanner on the market that may soon gain popularity due to its small, portable size.

- **Photo Scanners** are specially designed to scan photos, slides and negatives. If you intend to scan photographic slides, as well as text and graphics, look for a flatbed model that includes a transparency adapter or offers one as an add-on.

- **Multifunction Scanner/Printer/Fax** is an all-in-one device that saves space and alleviates the need for each device to be purchased separately. When choosing this form of device, make sure the printer is capable of printing in PostScript for document scalability (decreasing the document size).

IMPORTANT CONSIDERATIONS

- **Resolution**—usually the higher the number the sharper the scans. This is especially important when scanning photos, slides and negatives.

- **Color Depth**—sees the variations of colors. Shading and detail are improved significantly when the scanner reads as much color information as possible, during the original scanning process. For example, a 36-bit can distinguish between billions of color variations; a 48-bit can distinguish trillions.

- **Scan Area**—a large scan area allows scanning of large books, maps, drawings, paintings and newspapers. Be sure to determine your primary media to be scanned so that the scanner can accommodate.

- **Scan Head Technology**—

  1. **CIS** (Contact Image Sensor)—is smaller and can be slower.

  2. **CCD** (Charge-Coupled Device)—is more common and provides better quality scans. It can be faster especially if it has its own power source.

- **Connecting the Scanner**—most scanners are equipped with a variety of interfaces to match the computer. By far, USB is the easiest interface to install and fast enough for smaller jobs.

- **Document Feeder**—is good if you intend to scan many pages of documents at a time.

BRANDS

Like any product, brand reputation is important. HP, Canon, Epson, Microtek and Visioneer are some of the more reputable brands.

18

Choosing a Digital Camera

Besides looking at how many mega-pixels a camera has, also look at—like everything else—how you intend to use the camera. Action shots or still shots, do you intend to carry the camera often or only when going on weekly outings? A camera too slow may take too much time between shots, causing you to miss the best action. If the camera is too heavy, you may be less inclined to carry it regularly. When choosing a digital camera, things to keep in mind include the camera's **mega-pixels, resolution, size, focus range, storage capacity, battery life** and **screen**.

FEATURES TO KEEP IN MIND

- **Mega-pixels**

  Digital camera buyers believe that when it comes to mega-pixels, more is better. But that's not always the case. Cameras with more mega-pixels produce larger, crisp images. The tradeoff is that those images take up so much space. You may be able to store only a dozen (or fewer) images in the camera's memory. Moreover, if your camera can capture more mega-pixels, the resolution of your images measured in pixels will be higher, and you'll be able to produce larger high-quality prints.

  A 2-megapixel camera can produce images of about 1600 by 1200 pixels, allowing for high-quality 5-by-7 prints. A 3-megapixel camera can produce images of about 2048 by 1536 pixels, allowing for crisp 8-by-10 prints.

  If you're interested in producing mostly small snapshots or images to send via e-mail or post on the Web, you probably don't need anything bigger than a 2-megapixel camera. If you want to create large copies of your masterworks, you'll want a camera that captures 3-megapixels or more.

- **Resolution**

  A digital camera of any resolution will do if you intend to take pictures only to e-mail them to others or to create snapshots. However, more pixels give you greater flexibility allowing you to print sharper pictures at larger sizes, or crop and print small sections of pictures. A 2-megapixel camera can usually produce a pretty 5-by-7 print; a 3-megapixel camera, an 8-by-10; and a 4-megapixel model, an 11-by-17.

- **Size**

  Some users may consider a camera's weight and whether it fits in a pocket more important factors than resolution. Small cameras are convenient, but they frequently have tiny dials and buttons that can make changing settings difficult. Bigger cameras may have more powerful features but the heavy weight may discourage many.

- **Focal Range**

  Cameras with a greater focal range can take a range of photos from wide-angle to close-ups. Optical zoom produces sharper images than digital zoom. Many vendors, however, exaggerate this rating by combining the optical zoom (which moves the lens to magnify the subject) with digital zoom, which merely captures fewer pixels and magnifies them.

- **Storage Capacity**

  This measures the amount of data, in megabytes, the camera can store in its on-board memory, removable memory cards, or both. If you intend to shoot many pictures this could become an important consideration. Keep in mind, however, that the number of photos you can store depends on the resolution at which you shoot. At its highest resolution, a typical 2-megapixel camera can store eight to ten images on a 8MB memory card.

  Many cameras can capture video as well as still shots, though memory cards don't hold much video footage; the option is useful for short clips when you don't have a camcorder.

- **Battery Life**

  Digital cameras quickly drain batteries—especially alkaline batteries. Yet some cheap cameras have great battery life, and some expensive ones use up a charge quickly.

- **Screen**

  Screens are often good for reviewing just-taken images and are usually of the LCD variety. Low-end models often omit a LCD screen. LCD quality varies widely, many can wash out in sunlight or become grainy in low light, or the image may change if you tilt the camera slightly. If you can, try a camera outside before you buy.

BRANDS

Some of the more notable brands within the digital camera market include Sony, Canon, Minolta, Nikon, Epson, Kodak, HP, Olympus and Fuji.

PART VII
Too Much of a Good Thing

19

Avoiding Computer-Related Injuries

Computer use can be linked to a variety of **Repetitive Strain Injuries. Carpal Tunnel Syndrome (CTS)** and upper back and neck strains are common complaints from users who spend extended hours working at a computer. A few tips are included below, yet keep in mind a few tips cannot provide everything you need to know to prevent or reduce injury. If you feel you are suffering from a computer-related injury or have questions and concerns, see a qualified health professional.

Positioning	Keyboard	Mouse	Monitor
Choose a Chair Providing Lower Back Support Adjust chair so the seat does not press into the back of your knees Keep wrists Straight While Typing	Type with a light touch keeping your hands and fingers relaxed Split Keyboards help provide comfort and keep wrists and arms aligned while typing	Hold the mouse with a relaxed hand trying not to grip tightly Optical mice require no cleaning and are faster and more accurate, as a result less wrist activity is needed to move the cursor	Position Your Monitor so that the top of the screen is near eye level (bi-focal wearers may need to lower the screen or talk to a health professional about glasses for computer work)
Use a Footrest if your feet do not rest comfortably on the floor Center Your Monitor in front of you	Type with hands and wrists floating above the keyboard so that you are able to easily reach for distant items	The Trackball uses a ball for cursor movement and significantly reduces wrist movement since users roll fingers over the ball rather than use the wrist or hand	Place the monitor at about arms length and tilt it slightly downward to decrease glare from overhead lighting Adjust Resolution, font, brightness to a level comfortable to you
Place Keyboard and pointing device at elbow level and at your center Those with chronic hand and wrist pain may require a foot-operated mouse	Vendors include: Adesso DataDesk Microsoft Logitech Kensington Contour Designs IOGEAR Gyration	Vendors include: Adesso DataDesk Microsoft Logitech Kensington Contour Designs IOGEAR Gyration	Incorporate Monitor Stands and anti-glare filters if necessary 3M is a recognized manufacturer of filters that reduce glare and radiation

20

The Future of Computer Technology

What is it Called?	What Does it Do?	When Will it Arrive?	Problems?
Araphone	A faster data interface that can move data up to 200MB per second between the CPU and added device	Early 2004	PC Makers will have to support the new standard which could increase PC costs
Hyper-threading	Puts the idle parts of the computer processor to use. Especially useful for servers and hardcore multi-taskers	It's here	Supported by Windows XP and Linux, yet most software is not written to support Hyper-threading
Corporate Instant Messaging	Allow individuals to communicate in real-time. Can exchange files, conduct audio or video conferences and collaborate on projects	It's here	Will need a set standard so that different messengers can communicate. Instant messaging could have both a positive and negative impact on worker productivity
Presence Technology	Will let you know when your friends and colleagues are online. It will also let you know what device the person is using—PC, PDA or cell phone.	It's here. However, the service has not yet been implemented	You may have to pay to be left alone and remain unlisted
TabletPC	A handheld PC with handwriting and speech recognition capabilities, storage and transmission of handwritten notes and voice output.	It's here and readily available.	The small size will make it easy to steal or lose. Don't put important documents on these devices.
Magnetic RAM	Much sturdier and faster memory allowing you to turn off your computer without the loss of data.	Sometime in 2004	Still very expensive

(The Future of Computer Technology, continued)

What is it Called?	What Does it Do?	When Will it Arrive?	Problems?
DNA Computing	Solves extremely difficult problems by using the language of DNA, can store and execute enormous quantities of data and is extremely energy-efficient	Conceived by Dr. Leonard Adelman at USC. Currently in its infancy	Hold onto your secret data because the DNA computer will crack secret codes without a problem. Currently DNA Computing is too prone to errors
Broadband over Power Lines	Electric Power Lines used to deliver electric power to your home will also deliver broadband Internet access	Still in the testing phase. Some test areas have been using since the Summer of 2003. Otherwise 3 to 5 years away—or more.	Could be a tough battle to finally get the technology in wide use due to regulatory standards
Wearable Computer	Computers small enough to be worn on the body	It's here. A company called Xybernaut produces them	Could become a nuisance much like Cell Phones
Holographic Storage	Mega-Storage capacity capable of storing more than 900GB of data which could fit on a crystal the size of a sugar cube	Still under development. Could occur as far down the line as 2010	Very volatile technology in need of major research, simply reading data from the medium tends to erase the stored data

Credit Card-Size Hard Drive	A card the size of a credit card allowing you to save from 100MB to 5GB of data	Available since the second half of 2003.	Due to spinning parts inside the card, could experience problems similar to large-sized hard drives.
AFC Hard Drives	Antiferromagnetically Coupled Media. Also called "pixie dust", which allow hard drive makers to fit 20gigabits of information per square inch. Making a 400GB hard drive possible	The technology is already here but there is no demand for such large capacities	Such big drives will need newer technologies to access the data quickly which could increase the cost
Pentium 5 (Nehalem Chip)	Will be the newest processor made by Intel with better power management and 6GHz of speed	Between the end of 2003 to early 2005	A good cooling system must be made to contain such high speeds
Ultra Wideband (UWB)	A wireless technology for transmitting digital data over a wide frequency spectrum at a high rate.	1 to 2 years away	Technology may cause disruptions with other radio bands

PART VIII
Linux

21

Linux

When starting up the Linux operating system you will either start in the **graphical environment**—the use of icons—or in the **console environment**—the use of the command prompt. **NOTE: command prompt and shell prompt will be used interchangeably.**

If you choose the graphical method, once you enter the logon screen enter the appropriate username and password. You should have been asked to create this during the initial installation. If you only created a root account, enter that and then create a new account. It is a bad idea to use the root login as the main login since root has unlimited authority and the potential for you to unknowingly damage your system by deleting a needed component increases.

If you choose to login from the console, enter the user name and password at the prompt. Another prompt will follow, where you will enter **startx**. From here Linux starts the **X Windows** environment called **GNOME**. The other environment is called **KDE**. Once in X Windows, the Linux experience can begin.

How to Start a Shell Prompt using GNOME (up to Version 7.3)

- Go to Linux Paw → Programs → System → GNOME Terminal

How to Start a Shell Prompt using GNOMW (version 8.0 and above)

- Click the Red Hat → System Tools → Terminal

How to Start a Shell Prompt Using KDE

- Go to KDE Main Menu → System → Shell

USING THE SHELL PROMPT TO CREATE A NEW ACCOUNT

NOTE: You must be root (administrator) to create a new account.

- Launch the shell prompt
- Once in the shell type *su—*
- When prompted for password type the root password
- Type *useradd*, then the name for the new account (e.g. *useradd john*)
- Next, add the password for the newly created account
- At the prompt type *passwd* and type the account name just created (e.g. *passwd john*)
- From here you will be prompted for the New Unix password, type in the desired password and press enter. You will then be prompted: all authentication tokens updated successfully. Keep in mind that Linux is case-sensitive.

USING THE GRAPHICAL ENVIRONMENT TO CREATE A NEW ACCOUNT

- Go to the Linux Start Paw or the Red Hat at the lower left corner of the screen
- Go to System Settings
- Got to Users and Groups
- Create the account

USER HOME DIRECTORY

Under Linux, each user has his or her own home directory in which personal settings and information are kept. This directory is created after a new account and password are created. Once the user logs in, this folder can be found on the desktop. Backing up data is made easy by simply copying all the contents of this folder.

SET LINUX TO DIAL-UP

- Go to the Linux Start Paw or the Red Hat at the lower left corner of the screen
- Go to Extras
- Go to Internet

- Go to KPPP
- Input the proper settings provided to your from the Service Provider

FINDING YOUR IP ADDRESS AT THE SHELL PROMPT

- Launch a Shell prompt
- Type *ifconfig* or*/sbin/ifconfig*
- Find the numbers after *inet addr:* to see IP Address

FINDING YOUR IP ADDRESS FROM THE GRAPHICAL ENVIRONMENT

- Go to the Linux Start Paw or the Red Hat at the lower left corner of the screen
- Go to Preferences
- Go to Information
- Go to Network Interfaces

SWITCHING BETWEEN KDE AND GNOME DESKTOPS USING THE GRAPHICAL ENVIRONMENT

- Go to the Linux Start Paw or the Red Hat at the lower left corner of the screen
- Go to Extras
- Go to System Settings
- Go to Desktop Switching Tool
- Click the desired desktop environment

Log out then log in for the new desktop to take effect.

SWITCHING BETWEEN KDE AND GNOME USING THE COMMAND LINE

- Start a Shell prompt
- Type *switchdesk*
- When the switchdesk graphic comes up choose the desired environment

PRINT (CAPTURE) THE SCREEN

- Go to the Linux Start Paw or the Red Hat at the lower left corner of the screen
- Go to Graphics
- Go to Screen Capture Program

PRINT (CAPTURE) THE SCREEN RED HAT 7.3 AND EARLIER

- Start a Shell prompt
- Type *import* and name the image (e.g. *import screenshot.jpg*)
- The cursor will change to a cross hair
- Click on the image you wish to capture and it will be saved to you home folder under the name you chose, *screenshot.jpg* as in the example above.

ACCESSING A FLOPPY DRIVE UNDER THE KDE DESKTOP ENVIRONMENT

- Right-click the Floppy Disk icon found on the desktop
- Choose Mount Volume

ACCESSING A FLOPPY DRIVE FROM THE SHELL PROMPT

- Start a Shell prompt
- Type *mount/mnt/floppy*

EJECTING A FLOPPY DISK UNDER THE KDE DESKTOP ENVIRONMENT

NOTE: Before you can eject it, the disk must be unmounted. The data is then written to the disk.

- Right-click the floppy disk icon found on the desktop
- Choose Unmount Volume

- Any data you wanted copied is then written to the disk
- Eject the disk

EJECTING A FLOPPY DISK
FROM THE SHELL PROMPT

- At the Shell prompt type *unmount/mnt/floppy*

ACCESSING A CD-ROM DRIVE
UNDER THE KDE ENVIRONMENT

- Right-click the CD-ROM icon found on the desktop
- Choose Mount Volume

ACCESSING A CD-ROM DRIVE
FROM THE SHELL PROMPT

- At the Shell prompt type *mount/mnt/cdrom*

EJECTING A CD-ROM
UNDER THE KDE DESKTOP ENVIRONMENT

- Right-click the CD-ROM icon found on the desktop
- Choose Unmount Volume
- Eject Disk

EJECTING A CD-ROM
FROM THE SHELL PROMPT

- At the Shell prompt, type *unmount/mnt/cdrom* and press enter
- Then type *eject/mnt/cdrom* to eject the disk

Burning CDs Using Linux

- Insert and mount a blank CD
- Go to the Linux Start Paw or the Red Hat at the lower left corner of the screen
- Go to Extras
- Go to System Tools
- Go to CD Writer

-or-

- Insert and mount a blank CD
- Go to the Linux Start Paw or the Red Hat at the lower left corner of the screen
- Go to Extras
- Go to System Tools
- Go to the K on CD Program

Installing Programs Under Linux Using non RPM Programs—*TAR.GZ*

NOTE: Installing programs requires root permission.

- Start a Shell prompt
- Enter *su* (root) and root password
- Download the program to your hard drive. For ease, you can make a directory called *downloads* (e.g. *mkdir downloads*)
- Next, uncompress and untar the program. The directory/*usr/src* is usually used for this.
- Type *cd/usr/scr*
- Locate the name and location of the file you downloaded and instruct Linux to uncompress it to the/usr/scr directory:

For example:/home/john/downloads/newprogram.*tar.gz*

- At the prompt type: *tar–xzvf/home/john/downloads/newprogram.tar.gz* then press Enter

If you use Netscape to download the file leave out the "*z*".

From the above example the letters have the following meaning:

x: untar the file

z: uncompress the file

v: verbose, gives step-by-step information of what is occurring

f: file to untar follows

- Once the program is untarred, it will create a directory within the/usr/src directory
- Type *ls* at the command prompt to view the contents in/usr/scr directory
- Find the file that was just untarred and type *cd* (e.g. *cd newprogram*)
- **Find the README file and INSTALL file and read the contents to get the installation instructions**

The installation process uses either **make**, **make install** commands or the **./configure**, **make**, **make install** commands. Often the method used to compile can be determined by looking at which files are found in the directory.

INSTALLING PROGRAMS UNDER LINUX *USING RPM*

RPM automates the process of upgrading programs, keeping track of installed programs, removal of programs, checking for program dependencies and of course installing programs.
NOTE: Installing programs require root permission

- Start a Shell prompt
- Enter *su* (root) and root password
- Find the program in RPM format to install
- At the Shell prompt type *rpm–ivh name of file.i386.rpm* (e.g. *rpm–ivh mynewdownload-1.2.26.i386.rpm*)
- The program will install automatically

(Another method of installing RPM packages is by simply double-clicking the RPM packaged icon. The program will install automatically)

USING RPM FROM THE GNOME DESKTOP ENVIRONMENT

- Go to the Linux Start Paw or the Red Hat at the lower left corner of the screen
- Go to System
- Go to GnoRPM
- Select the Packages you wish to install
- Click the Install button

UNINSTALLING RPM PACKAGES

- Start a Shell prompt
- Type *rpm–e package name* (e.g. *rpm–e mynewdownload*)

NOTE: When uninstalling a package using RPM, only the name of the package is used instead of the complete file name.

COMMON RPM COMMANDS AND MEANINGS

rpm–i: installs a package
rpm–e: erases a package
rpm–U: upgrades a previously installed package
rpm–q: queries the database of installed packages
rpm–F: freshens or upgrades an already upgraded package
rpm–V: verifies a package
rpm–v: used in conjunction with other commands, displays progress and errors

To find the various RPMs installed on your system, go to the */var/lib/rpm* directory.

FINDING THE RUNNING PROCESSES AND PROGRAMS ON YOUR LINUX SYSTEM USING *TOP*

- Start a Shell prompt
- Type *top*
- All running processes and programs will be displayed with a **ProcessID (PID)**
- Type *q* to exit

STOPPING A STUBBORN OR HUNG PROCESS OR PROGRAM

- Start a Shell prompt
- Use the *top* utility as mentioned above
- Note the PID of the stubborn or hung program
- Type *q* to exit *top*
- Then type *kill PID* (e.g. *kill 211*)

FINDING THE SIZE OF A DIRECTORY

- Start a Shell prompt
- Type *du–h directory name* (e.g. *du–h/home/john*)

FINDING THE SPACE AVAILABLE ON THE DISK-DISK FREE

- Start a Shell prompt
- Type *df–h*

CONFIGURING THE DATE AND TIME

- Go to the Linux Start Paw or the Red Hat at the lower left corner of the screen
- Go to System Settings
- Go to Date & Time

Adjust the Date and Time appropriately. **NOTE The time uses the 24-hour format yet will display in standard format. If your computer is connected to the Internet, you can Enable Network Time Protocol.**

TEXT EDITORS

Text editors allow you to make modifications to Linux system files. To access text editors start a command prompt and simply type the name of the respective editor, e.g., pico, vi, vim, emacs. Keep in mind, however, that not all editors are installed on your Linux system by default. Emacs, vi, and pico are standard on many Linux distributions.

EDITING FILES WITH TEXT EDITORS

- Start a Shell prompt
- Type the name of the text editor you wish to use, e.g. *pico*
- Type the name of the file where the information to edit is found, e.g. */etc/inittab*
- *pico/etc/inittab* press Enter and make the appropriate changes
- Save the changes and exit out of the editor

NOTE: Make certain you know what you are doing when editing system files, system instability could result.

EDITORS

Graphical Editors	Basic Less Featured	Versatile, Less Powerful	Versatile and Powerful	Versatile, Powerful and Full-featured
gedit gless kedit kwrite	ee	ed pico nedit mcedit	sed jed joe	emacs vi vim

SHELL PROMPT COMMANDS

There are many Linux shell prompt commands. Below are the most commonly used commands allowing you to complete a variety of tasks. Most Linux commands have what are called the **man** pages to gain more insight into the command. This can be accomplished by typing **man** *command name* (e.g., *man chmod*) at the shell prompt. Included below is a chart of commands. Keep in mind that the majority of Linux commands are case-sensitive. Type **exit** to exit the command prompt.

Command prompt commands to launch configuration tools—Newer Versions of Red Hat

- Launches tool to configure Time and Date

  redhat-config-date

- Launches tool to configure Mouse

  redhat-config-mouse

- Launches tool to configure Monitor settings and Screen Resolution

  redhat-config-xfree86

- Launches tool to configure Network

  redhat-config-network

- Launches tool to Install or Remove Packages (programs) after installation

  redhat-config-packages

- Launches tool to configure the Firewall (security level)

  redhat-config-securitylevel

- Launches tool to configure Users and Passwords

  redhat-config-users

- Launches tool to configure specific Languages

  redhat-config-language

- Launches tool to configure the Sound card

redhat-config-soundcard

Command	Meaning	Example
ls	Lists Files	ls
ls –a	Lists all files	ls -a
ls –l	Lists file size	ls –l
ls --color	Adds color	ls --color
ls –S	Lists files by size	ls -S
clear	Clears screen	clear
exit	Closes prompt	exit
mv	Moves files	**mv** *file1.txt /home/john/documents*
mv	Renames a file	**mv** *file1.txt file1a.txt*
cp	Copies files	**cp** *file1a.txt /home/john/documents*
cp –l	Makes a shortcut	cp –l
cp –u	Copies if source is newer than destination	cp –u
cp –P	Copies directories and contents of subdirectories	cp –P
cp –I	Prompts for verification. Copies interactively	cp –i
rm	Deletes a file(s)	**rm** *file1a.txt*
mkdir	Creates a directory	**mkdir** *downloads*
pwd	Displays your location	pwd
cd	Changes from one directory location to another	**cd** */home/john/downloads*
cd ..	Changes to last directory	cd ..

Command	Meaning	Example
date	Displays and/or sets date	date
free	Shows how much RAM in use	free
grep	Finds a text or a string of text in a file	**grep** (whatever word or phrase) *file1a.txt*
diff	Compares the data of files	**diff** *file1a file1b*
su	Root user/Super user	su
su -	Root user with extra features	su -
whoami	Tells you which user you are logged on as	whoami
1a. shutdown –r now	Restarts computer	**shutdown** *–r now*
1b. reboot	Restarts computer	reboot
shutdown –h now	Shuts down computer	**shutdown** *–h now*
halt	Shuts down computer	halt
top	Views running programs and process in memory	top
/etc/init.d/<service> start	Starts or stops a service	*/etc/init.d/httpd* **start**
uname –a	Gives Linux Kernel Version and machine name	uname –a
mkbootdisk –device /dev/fd0 <kernel version>	Makes a Linux boot disk	**mkbootdisk** –device /dev/fd0 1.2332.linux
lpr	Used for Printing	**lpr** *filename*
man	Lists command instructions	**man** *command name*
mke2fs	Formats a diskette	*/sbin/mke2fs/dev/fd0*
ssh	Secure Shell, used to securely connect to a remote control	ssh *remotehostname or IP address*
---scp	Retrieve files from a remote computer	scp *remotehost:file1a*
---scp	Copies a file to a remote computer	scp *file1a remotecomputer:file1a*
sftp	SecureFTP, Transfers files with computer you can ssh	sftp
---get	Gets a file from remote computer	**get** *file1a*
---put	Places a file on a remote computer	**put** *file1a*

NOTE: When using ssh be sure that you know the username and password or have an account set on the computer you are connecting to. Otherwise, ssh will not allow you to connect to the computer.

CHANGING PERMISSIONS ON FILES, FOLDERS, AND PROGRAMS

There are two techniques you can use to change permissions while using Linux. The first is to right-click the file or program for which you wish to change permission and make the adjustments accordingly. The second and more advanced technique is to start a command prompt and use the **chmod** command.

chmod

Allows for changing of permissions on files, programs, and directories.

chmod owner reference

u: The owner of the file (you)

g: The group that the user belongs

o: All others

a: Everyone

chmod symbolic permissions

r: Permission to Read a file

w: Permission to Write to a file

x: Permission to eXecute a file

chmod symbols

+: Adds the permission

-: Removes the Permission

=: Sets the permission

chmod numerical values

4: Permission to Read

2: Permission to Write

1: Permission to Execute

0: No Permission

Owner, Group and Others Schematic

(rw-) (rw-) (r--) is the same as (4+2+0) (4+2+0) (4+0+0)

This example says that the Owner and Group has read and write access, the Others have only read access. **The order is understood to always be Owner, Group, and all Others.**

chmod use for Directories

-R: Set permissions for directory trees

chmod examples

g+w: adds group write access (e.g. *chmod g+w document1a.txt*)

o-x: removes execution access for all others (e.g. *chmod o-x document1a.txt*)

a+rwx: all everyone read, write and execution access (e.g., *chmod a+rwx document1a.txt*)

g=r: allows the group only read access (e.g. *chmod g=r document1a.txt*)

-R o=rwx: Allows only the owner read, write and execution directory access
(e.g. *chmod–R o=rwx downloads*)

chmod examples using numerical values

600 = (rw-) (---) (---): The owner is the only person with read and write access
(e.g. *chmod 600 file1a.txt*)

644 = (rw-) (r--) (r--): The owner has read and write access, the group has read access and all others have read access.
(e.g. *chmod 644 file1a.txt*)

666 = (rw-) (rw-) (rw-): The owner, group and all others have read and write access.
(e.g. *chmod 666 file1a.txt*)

700 = (rwx) (---) (---): The owner is the only person with read, write and execute access.
(e.g. *chmod 700 file1a.txt*)

744 = (rwx) (r--) (r--): The owner has read, write and execute access, the group and all others have only read access.
(e.g. *chmod 744 file1a.txt*)

777 = (rwx) (rwx) (rwx): Everyone has read, write, and execute access.
(e.g. *chmod 777 file1a.txt*)

chmod numerical values for directories

600 = (drw-) (---) (---): Only the owner can read and write to the directory.
(e.g. *chmod-R 600 downloads*—or—*chmod 600 dowloads*)

777 = (drwx) (drwx) (drwx): Allows everyone read, write and execution access to a directory.
(e.g. *chmod–R 777 downloads*—or—*chmod 777 downloads*)

UPGRADING LINUX

Upgrading Linux can be used to upgrade to a higher version (e.g. 8.0 to 9.0), or upgrade programs of the same version that were not previously installed. Upgrading Linux is just a matter of:

1. Insert the Linux installation CD

2. Restart the computer (the computer should startup the Linux operating system)

3. Go through the setup prompts

4. Choose Upgrade Existing System

5. Click Next (you should see an option that allows you to install specific packages, check that box if you wish to add programs (packages) not previously installed). Otherwise, proceed with the general upgrade.

FORMATTING A LINUX PARTITION

To format a Linux installation, use the first Linux installation disk and follow the steps as above but delete the partition when prompted. Or use the formatting techniques found later in this book using a Windows 95 or Windows 2000 floppy disk.

TOOLS TO ACCESS LINUX FROM THE WINDOWS OPERATING SYSTEM

There are a many tools available that allow Windows users to access a Linux machine. One such tool is the **ssh** client for Windows. With this client Windows users can access a Linux machine, provided there is an account set on the Linux machine that the Windows user has access to. Some common ssh clients include **PuTTY**, **WinSCP**, and **OpenSSH**. A powerful utility called **Cygwin** also gives Windows users an environment from which to connect to Linux machines and perform a variety of tasks.

All of these utilities are free and readily available for download online.

Another technique is to actually run the entire Linux operating system on top of Windows under a virtual console. Users can run Windows applications as normal and with the click of an icon on the Windows desktop start the Linux operating system. This is a good alternative if you wish to keep Windows as the main system without having to partition the hard drive. Some Virtual Machine software includes **vmware, wine, Win4Lin and VirtualPC**. Keep in mind, however, that the more memory your computer has, the faster these virtual machines will run.

TOOLS TO ACCESS LINUX FROM THE MACINTOSH OPERATING SYSTEM

The Macintosh OS X operating system has a built in BSD Unix Terminal (Command Prompt) that allows the input of Unix commands. Also, with the click of the mouse, OS X can be enabled to accept **ssh** connections. This is found under Sharing and choosing allow incoming ssh connections.

Using software called **Mac-on-Linux** allows the running of Macintosh OS 7.5.2 to OS 10.2.4 on a Linux system.

LINUX INTERFACES

The following list shows the various Linux interfaces and how they are represented when using Linux.

Network Card:	eth0
Floppy Drive:	fd0
IDE Hard Drive:	hda (first hard drive)
	hdb (second hard drive)
	hda1 (first partition on first hard drive)
	hdb1 (first partition on second hard drive)
SCSI Hard Drive:	sda (first scsi hard drive)
	sdb (second scsi hard drive)
	sda1 (first partition on first scsi hard drive)
	sdb1 (first partition on second hard drive)
lp0:	Parallel Ports
psaux:	ps/2
ttyS0:	Serial Communications port

VARIOUS LINUX SYSTEM DIRECTORIES

The following list shows the various directories used by Linux and what is stored in these directories.

/bin/—stores user commands

/sbin/—stores system commands

/root/—home directory of the root user

/mnt/—stores mount points after system boots

/boot/—stores files used for startup

/lost+found/—used by fsck to place files without names

/lib/—contains library files that are used by programs

/dev/—stores device files

/etc/—stores configuration files and directories

/var/—stores files that change like the printer spool

/usr/—stores files and directories relating to users

/proc/—contains system information used by some programs, a virtual file system

/initrd/—stores files used to mount images needed load during startup

/tmp/—temp directory for users and allows all users read and write access

/home/—stores home directories for each user

/opt/—used to store files for installation and uninstallation of software

/sbin/shadow—stores shadow passwords if enabled. Can only be accessed by root

SOME LINUX CHOICES

Below is a small list of the various Linux distributions available. I say small because there are more than 100 to choose from. These, however, are the most commonly used.

Caldera <http://www.calderasystems.com/> Geared towards businesses. Touted as the easiest Linux installation.

Conectiva <http://www.conectiva.com/> The most popular distributions in Latin America.

Corel Linux <http://linux.corel.com/> Similar yet easier than Debian.

Debian <http://www.debian.org/> Primarily maintained by developers.

Linux PPC <http://www.linuxppc.com/> For the PowerPC architecture.

Mandrake <http://www.linux-mandrake.com/en/> A Red Hat based distribution optimized for the Pentium processor.

Red Hat <http://www.redhat.com/> The most popular Linux distribution of the USA.

Slackware <http://www.slackware.com/> Oldest Linux distribution. Geared towards advanced users, with Unix-like functionality.

SuSE <http://www.suse.com/> The most popular Linux distribution of Europe, also, one of the biggest installations.

TurboLinux <http://www.turbolinux.com/> The most popular Linux distribution of Asia.

Yellow Dog Linux <http://www.yellowdoglinux.com/> A distribution for the PowerPC architecture. Good for the MacintoshG3 or G4.

Smoothwall Linux <http://www.smoothwall.org/> Good for creating a firewall.

Black Cat Linux <http://www.blackcatlinux.com/> Based on Red Hat with support for Russian and Ukranian languages.

KSI Linux <http://www.ksi-linux.com> Supports Russian, English and Ukrainian languages.

Phat Linux <http://www.phatlinux.com/> A Linux in Windows distribution.

ROCK Linux <http://linux.rock-projects.com/> Designed for highly skilled Linux Users and Administrators.

Storm Linux <http://www.stormix.com/> Good for networks.

tomsrtbt: <http://www.toms.net/rb/home.html> A full featured one (1) disk bootable Linux floppy.

Trinux <http://www.trinux.org> 2–3 disk Linux distribution that runs in RAM and contains the latest network security and monitoring tools.

UltraPenguin <http://ultra.penguin.cz/> Based on Red Hat for SPARC and UltraSPARC Workstations.

WinLinux2000 <http://www.winlinux.net/> Operates using a windows-based interface.

PART IX
Doing Things

22

Customizing Internet Options

LOCATION OF BOOKMARKS

Using a PC

- **Internet Explorer**. To find your Internet Explorer Bookmarks double-click **My Computer** → double-click **C:** → Go to **Documents and Settings** find your profile name. Within your profile you will find a file called **Favorites** this is where all of your Internet Explorer Bookmarks are kept. This file can be copied to a floppy disk, or elsewhere, for safekeeping and backup.

- **Netscape**. To locate Netscape Bookmarks double-click **My Computer** → double-click **C:** → Go to **Program Files** → **Netscape**. Within the Netscape folder you will see a folder called **Users**, double-click this folder and go to the name of your profile, otherwise go to the folder named **default**. Within this folder you will see a file called **bookmark.htm**. This little file contains all of your Netscape bookmarks. This file can be copied to a floppy disk, or elsewhere, for safekeeping and backup.

Using a Mac OS X

- **Internet Explorer**. To locate Internet Explorer Bookmarks go to the **Hard Drive icon** → **Users** → **find your profile name** → **Library** → **Preferences** → **Explorer** → select the **Favorites.html** file. This file will contain all of your existing Internet Explorer bookmarks. This file can be copied to a floppy disk, or elsewhere, for safekeeping and backup.

- **Netscape**. To locate Netscape Bookmarks go to **the Hard Drive icon** located on the desktop → **Users** → **find your profile name** → **Library** → **Mozilla** → **Profiles** → **find the name you gave your Netscape profile** → **go to the Folder following your profile name, which may be a series of numbers and letters** → find **bookmarks.html**. This file can be copied to a floppy disk, or elsewhere, for safekeeping and backup.

Using a Mac OS 9.x

- **Internet Explorer**. To locate Internet Explorer Bookmarks go to **the Hard drive icon** → **System Folder** → **Preferences** → **Explorer** → copy **Favorites.html** to a floppy disk, or elsewhere, for safekeeping and backup.

- **Netscape**. To locate Netscape Bookmarks go to **the hard drive icon** → **System Folder** → **Preferences** → **Netscape Users** → choose the name you gave your Netscape profile → copy **Bookmarks.html** to a floppy disk, or elsewhere, for safekeeping and backup.

FINDING AND DELETING WEB SITE HISTORY AND DELETING COOKIES (PC)

Cookies and web site history are small bits of data placed on your computer by some Web sites. They contain your personal information, like the passwords and login names used for the web site, last web pages visited and/or the date you last visited the site.

NETSCAPE

Launch Netscape → go to **Edit** → **Preferences** → under the **Category** column click the **Navigator** tab. Go to **History** → click **Clear History**

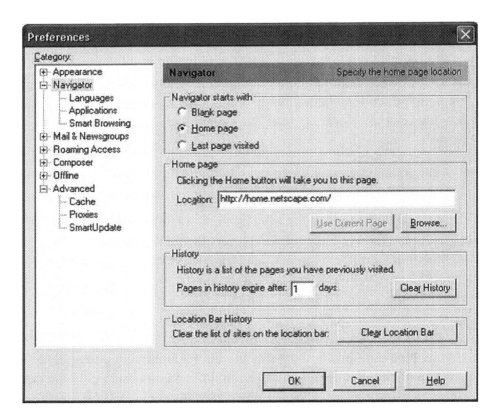

Deleting Cookies

NETSCAPE

Double-click the **My Computer icon** → go to **Program Files** → double-click the **Netscape** folder → double-click the **Users** folder → find your profile name (or choose **default** if you are the only user) → look for a file named **Cookies** and **delete** it. Click **OK**.

INTERNET EXPLORER

Launch Internet Explorer → across the top go to **Tools** → **Internet Options…**→ select the **General** tab → under the **Temporary Internet Files** section click **Delete Cookies** also click **Delete Files…**(some browsers only have the Delete Files…button). Click the **Settings…**button → click **View Files…**→ select all of the cookies by holding down the **Ctrl** and then the **A** key together. Press **Delete**. Click **Yes**. Click **Apply** → **OK**.

Go to **Advanced** → scroll to the **Security** setting →check **Empty Temporary Files folder when browser is closed.** → **Apply** → **OK**

Deleting other Web Site Information from Your Hard Drive

NETSCAPE

Launch Netscape → go to **Edit** → **Preferences** → in the Category column go to → **Advanced** → choose **Cache** → click **Clear Memory Cache** and **Clear Disk Cache**. Click **OK**.

INTERNET EXPLORER

Launch Internet Explorer → across the top go to **Tools** → **Internet Options…**→ select the **General** tab → under the **History** section click **Clear History**.

Stop AutoComplete of Web pages

INTERNET EXPLORER

Choose the **Content** Tab → click **AutoComplete…**uncheck **Web addresses**. (You will find other useful tools under the AutoComplete tab)

NETSCAPE

Go to **Edit** → **Preferences…**→ under Category: choose **Navigator** → choose **Smart Browsing** → uncheck **Enable Internet Keywords** or uncheck Internet Keyword AutoComplete depending on the version of Netscape.

Finding and Deleting Web Site History and Deleting Cookies (OS X)

Deleting Web Site History

INTERNET EXPLORER

To delete the record of the web sites you visited **Launch Internet ExplorerAt the top left corner click Explorer** → Scroll to **Preferences...**→ **Web Browser** → go to **Advanced** → go to **Cache** → click **Empty Now**

NETSCAPE

Launch **Netscape**→ go to **Edit** → **Preferences...**→ under the **Category** box, go to the **Navigator** tab → go to **History** → click **Clear History**

-and-

Under the **Category** box go to the **Advanced** tab → **Cache** → click **Clear Memory Cache** → click **Clear Disk Cache**

Deleting Cookies

INTERNET EXPLORER

Under the **Web Browser** box go to → **Receiving Files** → select **Cookies** select all of the cookies listed → click **Delete**

NETSCAPE

Under the **Category** box go to **Privacy & Security** → select **Cookies** → go to **View Stored Cookies** → go to the **Stored Cookies** tab → click **Remove All Cookies**

Finding and Deleting Web Site History and Deleting Cookies (OS 9.x)

Deleting Web Site History

INTERNET EXPLORER

Launch Internet Explorer → select **Edit** → scroll to **Preferences...**→ **Web Browser** go to **Advanced** → go to **Cache** → click **Empty Now**

NETSCAPE

Launch Netscape → go to **Edit** → **Preferences...**→ under the **Category** box select **Navigator** → go to **History** → click **Expire Now**

-and-

Under the **Category** box go to **Advanced** → **Cache** → click **Clear Disk Cache Now**

Deleting Cookies

INTERNET EXPLORER

Under the **Web Browser** box go to **Receiving Files** → select **Cookies** → select all of the cookies listed → click **Delete**

NETSCAPE

Double-click the **Hard Drive icon** → Double-click the **System Folder** → Double-click the **Preferences Folder** → Double-click the **Netscape Users** folder → Double-Click the **Profile Folder** and choose the name of your profile → In this folder you will find a file called **Magic-Cookie** → *(drag the MagicCookie file to the trash)*—or—single-click the MagicCookie file so that it is highlighted → go to **File** → choose **Move To Trash**

23

Burning CDs and DVDs

USING ADAPTEC EASY CD CREATOR (WINDOWS)

Start up **Easy CD Creator** → **Start** → **Programs** → **Roxio Easy CD Creator** → **Project Selector** → **Make A Data CD** → go to **Data CD Project** → find the data you wish to copy to CD by selecting **Select Source Files** → once you have found the data you wish to copy, click the **Add** button.

NOTE: If you wish to remove any data that you added, click the Remove button. The data will not be deleted from the computer rather removed from the CD burning project.

Once you have all of the data you wish to burn, click the **Record** button.

NOTE: CD-R discs cannot be erased.

CREATING A MULTI-SESSION CD

A **multisession** CD allows you to add new data to a CD at later times or make musical compilations of different CDs. In order to do this, you must configure the CD burning software beforehand.

USING ROXIO EASY CD CREATOR

After you have added the tracks or tack to be copied click **Record** → click **Options** → under the **Record Method** check **Track-At-Once** and **Finalize Session. Don't Finalize CD.**

To add additional data at a later time follow the same procedure.

NOTE: A multi-session music CD is not recommended because only the tracks recorded in the first session are playable.

ERASING A CD-RW DISC

Insert CD-RW → Start up Easy CD Creator→ Select **Data CD** → go **Disc** → scroll to **Erase Disc**.

BURNING A DATA DVD

NOTE: You must have a DVD-R/RW or DVD+R/RW drive to record DVD discs. Also, make sure the DVD disc supports your DVD-R/RW or DVD+R/RW drive.

Go to **Start** → **Programs** → **Roxio Easy CD Creator** → **Project Selector** Choose **make a data CD** → go to **dataDVD project** → under **Select source files:** choose the files and/or folders you wish to copy → click the **Add** arrow → once you have added all of the data you wish to record. Click **record**

USING DIRECT CD

Easy CD Creator **Direct CD** allows you to copy data directly to a recordable CD or recordable DVD. Insert a blank CD-R/RW or DVD-R/RW +R/RW → go to **Start** → **Programs** → **Roxio Easy CD Creator** → **Applications** → **DirectCD Format Utility**

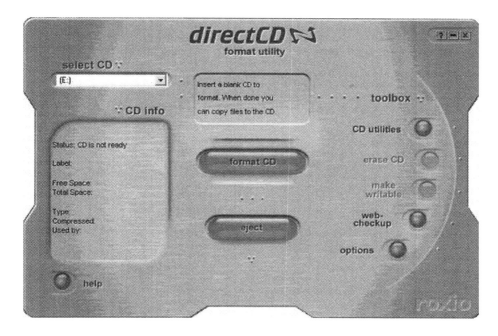

Select **format CD**. Once the CD is formatted, you will be able to copy data directly to the Disc. The Disc will show up in My Computer as another drive letter. To view it, double-click the **My Computer** icon.

To start copying data to the disc simply select the data using the **left mouse button**, continue to hold the left mouse button while dragging the data you want copied to the new drive, once there, release the left mouse button—the data will then be copied to the disc.

You can also **right-click** the data you want copied and select **Send To**, scroll to **DirectCD Drive**, the data will be copied to the disc.

Check out the following link for more information on using Roxio Easy CD Creator:

http://support.ap.dell.com/docs/software/roxio5/en/

ERASING A DVD

NOTE: you cannot erase a DVD-R or DVD+R disc.

Insert the DVD-RW or DVD+RW disc → go to the **dataDVD project** → across the top, go to **Disc** → select **Erase Disc**.

APPLE'S BUILT-IN DISC CREATOR

Apple iTunes

iTunes is Apple's music program that allows users to listen to live music and radio streams from the Internet, the user can also play precompiled music from the hard drive or from music CDs.

Converting a Disc to MP3 using Apple's iTunes

Launch iTunes → across the top go to **Advanced** → choose **Convert Selection to MP3**.

Apple's Built-in Disc Burner

Apple has a disc-burning program that comes standard with its CD-R/RW capable computers. **Disc Burn** allows you to easily create your own data CDs. Burning CDs is a matter of inserting a blank disc, selecting the format and dragging the contents on the disc icon found on the desktop. However, this program is not a specialized burning program. It does not allow the burning of CDs in a hybrid format such as HFS/ISO-9660/Joliet. As a result, Windows and Linux systems will have problems reading these disks. Also, multi-session burning is not supported. Purchasing CD Burning software will solve this, however. **Roxio Toast** is a popular CD Burning software for the Macintosh. The link below has some basic to advanced burning tips for Macs using **Toast**.

http://www.roxio.com/en/support/toast/knowledgebase.jhtml

Burning a Disc Using Disc Burn (OS X)

Insert the blank disc → **Format** the disc when prompted → disc icon will appear on the desktop → **drag-and-drop** files on the CD icon → click the **Burn** button found under the **Finder**.

WINDOWS XP BUILT-IN CD BURNING PROGRAM

If you have Windows XP and a CD Rewritable (CD-RW) or CD Recordable (CD-R) drive, you can burn photos, music, or other data to a CD.

To copy files and folders to a CD

1. Insert a blank CD into the CD recorder → double-click **My Computer**.

2. Click the files or folders you want to copy to the CD. To select more than one file, hold down the **CTRL** key while you click the files you want. Then, under **File and Folder Tasks**, click **Copy this file**, **Copy this folder**, or **Copy the selected items**.If the files are located in **My Pictures**, under **Picture Tasks**, click **Copy to CD** or **Copy all items to CD**, and then skip to step 5.

3. In the **Copy Items** dialog box, click the CD recording drive, and then click **Copy**.

4. In **My Computer**, double-click the CD recording drive. Windows displays a temporary area where the files are held before they are copied to the CD. Verify that the files and folders that you intend to copy to the CD appear under **Files Ready to be Written to the CD**.

5. Under **CD Writing Tasks**, click **Write these files to CD**. Windows displays the **CD Writing Wizard**. Follow the instructions in the wizard.

Be sure that you have enough disk space on your hard disk to store the temporary files that are created during the CD writing process. For a standard CD, Windows reserves up to 700 MB of the available free space. For a high-capacity CD, Windows reserves up to 1 gigabyte (GB) of the available free space.

BURNING A MUSIC CD (WINDOWS XP)

Launch **Windows Media Player** → Insert the Music CD you wish to Copy → Across the top go to **View** → select **Full Mode** → place a check mark next to the music tracks you wish to copy → on the taskbar to the left, select **Copy from CD** (a legal disclaimer may appear, check the box provided to proceed) → at the top of the console click the red **Copy Music** button.

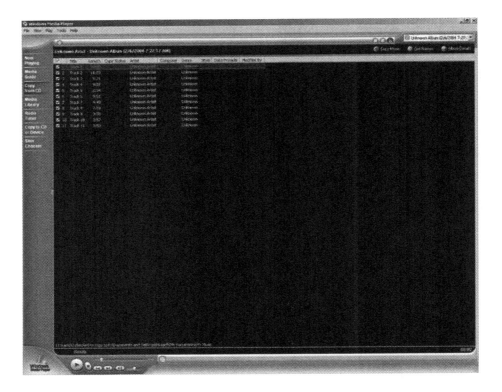

NERO BURNING ROM

Nero is another popular CD and DVD burning software. They have a comprehensive web site covering basic to advanced burning techniques located at the web address below:

http://www.nero.com/en/index.html#c1002822790847

24

Macintosh and Windows How-To

This how-to section is broken down into Views, Printing, Creating Accents and Special Characters and Adding Additional Languages, Windows Command Prompt Commands, Creating Shortcuts and Power Options, Miscellaneous, Problems and Diagnostic tools, and finally Upgrading, Re-installing, Formatting.

SECTION I. VIEWS

Find The Names and Types Of Programs Found on Your Computer (PC)

Go to **Start** → **Settings** → **Control Panel** → **Add/Remove Programs**. From here you will find the currently installed programs, the size in megabytes (MB) and how often used.

How to Remove a Program From Your Computer (PC)

Go to **Start** → **Settings** → **Control Panel** → **Add/Remove Programs**. Select the program that you wish to remove → click **Remove**.

How Do I See All of the Programs and Other Information on My Mac (OS X)?

Double-click the hard drive icon → go to **Applications** → **Utilities** → **Apple System Profiler**. From here you will come across a series of tabs allowing you to check the amount of **memory**, **network** information, **processor** information, **all installed software**, and **operating system** information.

How to Customize The way all of your Files and Folders are Viewed (PC)

Set the desired view by going to **My Computer** → across the top go to **Tools** → **Folder Options** → **View** → select the **Apply to All Folders** button. All of your folders will then have the same view each time.

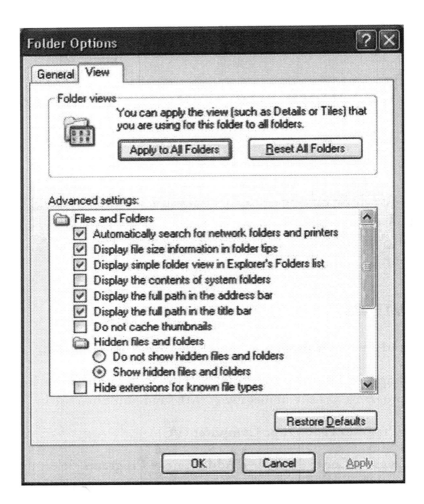

Checking the size of a File or Folder (PC)

Right-click the file or folder → scroll to **Properties** → view the **Size** in MB or GB

Checking the size of a File or Folder (Mac OS 9.x and OS X)

Single-click the file or folder → press and hold the **Control (Ctrl)** key and the **I** key → got to **Get Info** → scroll to **General Information** → view the **Size** in MB or GB.

SECTION II. PRINTING

How to assign one printer, of many, to be the default (PC)

Click the **Start** button → **Settings** → **Printers** → **Right-click** the desired printer → scroll to **Select as Default.**

How to assign one printer, of many, to be the default (Mac)

Double-click the printer alias on your desktop, a window for that printer will open. Across the top go to **Printing** → select **Set as Default Printer**

-or-

Go to Hard drive icon → **Applications** → **Utilities** → **Print Center** → click the printer you wish to be default → across the top choose Printing → select **Set as Default Printer**

Printing on both sides of the paper—duplex printing (PC)

Not all printers have the capacity to print on both sides of the paper.

When you are ready to print your document go to **File** → select **Print**, the Print dialog box opens. From the Print dialog box, select **Properties**.

Depending upon your operating system and driver type, select the duplex option using one of the following steps:

1. **Click** the **Finishing** tab, and in **Document Options**, select **Print on both sides.**

2. **Click** the **Page Setup** tab, and select either **Short Side <u>or</u> Long Side (NOTE the graphical representations of these two modes of duplexing).**

3. Select the **Paper** tab, and click **More Options**, then select either **Flip on long edge <u>or</u> Flip on short edge (NOTE the graphical representations of these two modes of duplexing).**

Printing on both sides of the paper—duplex printing (Mac)

Not all printers have the capacity to print on both sides of the paper.

When you are ready to print your document go to **Print** → click the General pop-up menu, and select **Layout**, the options in the dialog box will change → click **Print on Both Sides** check box → Click the **Print** button.

Cannot Print while using OS 9 applications under OS X

Go to the **Apple icon** at the top left corner—it should be the multi-colored apple icon → Go to **Chooser** → choose the **LASERWRITER** icon and add your printer. **Otherwise, you may need to startup in OS 9 and add the printer.** To do this:

Go to **Apple icon** → **System Preferences…**→ **Startup Disk** → select **Mac OS 9.2.2 (or other version)** → click **restart** → **Save and Restart**.

Follow the instructions to add a printer under OS 9 using the above method, installing printer drivers (software) if needed.

When done go to **Apple icon** → **Control Panels** → **Startup Disk** → choose **OS 10.2** → click **restart**.

When trying to print certain Word documents, I get an error message saying: "There is not enough memory in the printer."

This can occur if the printer is low on memory or if you are using a unique font not found in the printer. The font may either need to be loaded into the printer or the font may be corrupted requiring reloading. Printers found in offices usually have only the basic fonts and little memory. Yet, the printer may just not have enough memory to use the unique font, in this case only basic fonts should be used.

How To Create PDF Documents (PC)

1. Open the document

2. Choose **Print** from the File menu

3. In the Printer Name drop-down menu, choose **Acrobat PDFwriter**

4. You will be asked for a filename and a location to save the document

5. Choose the filename to save the document making sure it ends in **.pdf**

6. Close the document

7. Go to the location you chose to save the document and find it in its .pdf format.

How To Create PDF Documents (Mac)

NOTE: OS X has its own PDF client, yet you may opt to use Adobe Acrobat if you choose.

1. **Choose** File → Create PDF

2. Select the appropriate settings

3. Click **Create**.

NOTE: You can use the same technique to save web pages, jpeg files, and a host of other files as a PDF.

Difference between Adobe Acrobat Reader and Adobe Acrobat

Adobe Acrobat Reader is a free download that allows you to **open** PDF files. Adobe Acrobat (full version) is the paid version that allows you to **open** and **create** PDF documents.

SECTION III. CREATING ACCENTS AND SPECIAL CHARACTERS/ ADDING ADDITIONAL LANGUANGES

Accents and Special Characters for the Macintosh

To type accented characters and letters you must use special keystrokes.

To do this, you first hold down the keys (**Keys to Press Together**). Nothing will appear on your screen at this point. Release *both* keys, and *then* type the letter you would like to carry the accent (**Characters You Wish to Type**), as indicated below.

NOTE: DO NOT use the + key, it is there for clarity. Use what is before and after the +.

Characters You Wish to Type	Keys to Press Together
á, é, í, ó, ú	Option + E
à, è, ì, ò, ù	Option + ~
ä, ë, ï, ö, ü	Option + U
â, ê, î, ô, û	Option + I
ñ, ã, õ	Option + N
Ç	Option + C
Ç	Option + Shift + C
ß	Option + S
Æ	Option + '
¡	Option + ;
¿	Option + Shift + /
®	Option + R
©	Option + G
•	Option + 8
¶	Option + 7
€	Option + Shift + 2

Accents and Special Characters for Windows

Primarily, the **Ctrl** will be used to make the special characters and accents. This is done by holding down **Ctrl** and the **Shift** key.

To do this, you first hold down the keys **(Keys to Press Together)**. Nothing will appear on your screen at this point. Release *both* keys, and *then* type the letter you would like to carry the accent **(Characters You Wish to Type)**, as indicated below:

NOTE: A few accents and characters require an additional step. In addition, DO NOT use the + key, it is there for clarity. Use what is before and after the +.

Characters You Wish to Type	Keys to Press Together	
á, é, í, ó, ú	Ctrl + '	
à, è, ì, ò, ù	Ctrl + ~	
ä, ë, ï, ö, ü	Ctrl + Shift + ;	
â, ê, î, ô, û	Ctrl + Shift + 6	
ñ, ã, õ	Ctrl + Shift + ~	
ç, Ç	Ctrl + <	*then* Shift + C
Æ	Ctrl + Shift + 7	*then* A
oe, OE	Ctrl + Shift + 7	*then* Shift + O
¡	Alt + Ctrl + Shift + 1	
¿	Alt + Ctrl + Shift + /	
ø, Ø	Ctrl + /	*then* Ctrl + O
ß	Ctrl + Shift + 7	*then* S
å, Å	Ctrl + Shift + 2	*then* Shift + A
€	Alt + Ctrl + E	

Using Numbers to Create Special Characters and Accents (PC)

1. Make sure **Num Lock (Num Lk)** is on—located at the top left of the numerical keypad on the right side of the keyboard.

2. Hold down the **Alt** key and type the 3-digit numeric code for the special character using the chart below as a reference.

NOTE: You must type the 3-digit code on the numbered keypad. It will not work neither on the regular numbered keys above the letter keys nor on laptop keyboards. The special character will appear after you release the **Alt** key after typing the code.

â 131	Ç 128	ï 139	Ö 153
ä 132	ê 136	ì 141	û 150
à 133	ë 137	í 161	ü 129
á 160	è 138	ñ 164	ù 151
å 134	é 130	Ñ165	ú 163
Ä 142	É 144	ô 147	Ü 154
Å 143	æ 145	ö 148	ÿ 152
ß 225	Æ 146	ò 149	¿ 168
ç 135	î 140	ó 162	¡ 173

How to Add and Enable Additional Languages in Windows

The following links show the appropriate method to enable your computer to create documents and read documents in a foreign language.

<u>Using Windows</u>

This link shows the steps for language configuration for **Windows XP**

http://www.microsoft.com/windowsxp/pro/using/itpro/managing/regionalsup.asp

The following link shows the steps for language configuration for **Windows NT 4.0**, **Windows 2000** and **Windows XP**

http://support.microsoft.com/default.aspx?scid=kb;EN-US;177561

<u>Using Mac OS 9.x</u>

http://docs.info.apple.com/article.html?artnum=50037

<u>Using Mac OS X</u>

Go to the **Apple icon** → scroll to **System Preferences…**→ choose **International** → adjust the settings that meet your language requirement.

SECTION IV. WINDOWS COMMAND PROMPT COMMANDS

NOTE: Many of the commands do not work on all versions of Windows
Start > Programs > Accessories > Command Prompt to start the prompt—**or**—
Start > Programs > MSDOS

Command	Function
explorer	launches Windows Explorer
notepad	launches Notepad
regedit	launches the Windows Registry
winhelp	launches Windows Help
winhlp32	launches Windows help guides
accwiz	launches the Accessibility Wizard
calcs	File Permission utility
calc	launches the Calculator
certmgr.msc	launches Certificate Manager
charmap	launches Character Map
chkdsk	runs the Utility to check the hard drive (press **ctrl** and **x** to stop the Utility)
ciadv.msc	launches the Indexing service to change files and retrieve information from a set of documents
cipher	launches a command line utility that shows or changes the encryption
cleanmgr	launches the Cleanup utility
cliconfg	launches the SQL Server utility client Network Utility
clipbrd	launches the clipboard
comp	launches utility that compares the contents of two files or sets of files
compact	launches a compression/uncompression utility for files on NTFS partitions
compmgmt.msc	launches the computer management utility
control	launches the control panel
convert	launches convert utility for converting FAT files systems into NTFS
dcomcnfg	launches the Microsoft Management Console
ddeshare	launches DDE Share (Dynamic Data Exchange) to create, share and modify DDE shares with other computers
devmgmt.msc	launches the Device Manager
dfrg.msc	launches the Disk Defragmenter Utility
diskcomp	launches utility to compare contents of Floppy Disks
diskcopy	launches utility to copy information from one floppy disk to another
diskmgmt.msc	launches the disk management utility
dvdplay	launches the DVD/CD Player
dxdiag	launches the DirectX Diagnostic Tool
edit	launches the Windows Edit utility
esentutl	launches the Maintenance utility for Microsoft Databases
eudcedit	launches the Private Character Editor Utility
eventvwr	launches the Windows Event Viewer
expand	launches the utility to expand compressed files

(continued)

Command	Function
find	launches the utility that searches for a text string in a file or files
findstr	launches a utility that searches for strings in files
format	launches a utility to format disks
freecell	launches the FreeCell card game
fsmgmt.msc	launches the shared folders utility
ftp	launches the FTP protocol
gpedit	launches the Local Computer Policy utility
hostname	displays the computer's hostname
magnify	launches the Magnify utility to magnify text
mem	displays memory in use by the computer
mmc	launches the Microsoft Management Console
mobsync	launches the Synchronization utility
mspaint	launches the Microsoft Paint utility
ntmsmgr.msc	launches the Removable Storage Management Console
odbcad32	launches the ODBC Data Source Administrator
osk	launches the on-screen keyboard
pentnt	reports floating point errors
perfmon.msc	launches system performance monitor
progman	launches the Program Manager utility used to launch other programs
regsvr32	used to register dlls
replace	used to replace files
rsh	runs commands on remote hosts running the RSH service
secpol.msc	launches the Local Security Policy Manager
services.msc	launches the Services Console
sfc	scans protected system files and makes changes if needed
shrpubw	launches the Create Shared Folder utility
sndrec32	launches the Sound Recorder
sndvol32	launches the Volume Control
sol	launches the Solitaire card game
syskey	launches the Security tool to configure Accounts Database Security

(continued)

Command	Function
taskmgr	launches the Task Manager
tree	launches the System Tree
utilman	launches the Utility Manager
verifier	launches the Driver Verifier Manager
w32tm	launches the Time Manager
winchat	launches the Windows Chat Manager
winmine	launches the Windows Minesweeper game
write	launches WordPad
wupdmgr	launches web page to Microsoft updates
xcopy	copies files and directory trees
wbemtest	launches the Windows Management Instrumentation Tester
explorer mailto: me@yahoo.com	launches e-mail to send a message
winver	displays operating system version
explorer http://www.google.com	launches web browser
tsshutdn	shuts down a server
systeminfo	supplies information about a system or systems
syncapp	launches My Briefcase and adds a My Briefcase icon to the desktop to organize documents
spider	launches the spider card game
rtcshare	launches the sharing utility
recover	recovers readable information from a bad or defective disk
rasphone	launches the Network Connection utility
qprocess	displays information about running processes
qwinsta	displays information about Terminal Sessions
openfiles	lists and disconnects files and folders that are open
mstsc	launches the Remote Desktop utility
msg	sends a message to a user
mshearts	launches the Microsoft Hearts game
getmac	displays the MAC address for one or more network adapters on a system
tsdiscon	disconnects a Terminal session
tskill	ends a process
taskkill	ends one or more processes

SECTION V. CREATING SHORTCUTS AND POWER OPTIONS

Using The versatile ctrl (Control) key with the Macintosh (OS 9.x and OS X)

Use of the ctrl(Control) key allows for a number of different properties to take place. **Press and hold** the **ctrl(Control)** Key and → **single-click** documents, folders, mounted CDs or DVDs to make the following occur:

-Make an Alias
-Duplicate
-Open
-Eject
-Copy
-Get Info
-Help

How do I Make a Shortcut in the Dock (OS X)

Click the application's icon with your mouse, while holding the mouse button drag the icon to the dock. Once there, release the mouse. You can move the icon to any location in the dock by using your mouse. However, if you drag the icon to the desktop from the dock it will—"Poof"—delete the shortcut, and you will need to start the process again.

How do I Make a Shortcut on the Desktop (OS X)

The Macintosh calls shortcuts **Aliases**. Hold down the **ctrl (Control)** key → **click** the object you would like to be an alias → Scroll to **Make Alias**.

How do I Make a Shortcut on the Desktop (OS 9)

Press and hold the **ctrl (Control)** key → **click** the object you would like to be an alias → select **Make Alias** from the dialog box that appears.

How do I Make a Shortcut on the Desktop (PC)?

1. **Right-click** the object you would like to be a shortcut → scroll to **Create Shortcut**.

or

2. **Right-click** the object you would like to be a shortcut → scroll to **Send To** → select **Desktop (create shortcut)**.

How to Enable the Screen Saver (OS X)

Go to the **Apple icon** → **System Preferences** → **Screen Effects** → choose **Screen Saver Picture** → click the **Activation** tab → slide the tab to the desired time and choose whether you want a password to prompt you under the **Password to use when waking the screen effect**.

How to adjust the Energy Saver (OS X)

Go to the **Apple icon** → go to **System Preferences** → **Energy Saver** → click the **Sleep** tab → adjust to the appropriate settings to suit your needs.

How to adjust the Energy Saver (OS 9)

Go to the **Apple icon** → **Control Panels** → **Energy Saver** → click **Sleep Setup** and adjust to the appropriate settings that suit your needs. **NOTE: You can customize these settings by clicking the Show Details button**.

How to adjust the Screen Saver (OS 9)

Go to the **Apple icon** → **Control Panels** → **Appearance** → click the **Desktop** tab to adjust the desktop image.

Adjusting the Screen Saver Option (PC)

Go to the **Start** button → **Settings** → **Control Panel** → **Display** → **Screen Saver** → adjust the screen saver → enable **Password** protection if you wish.

Adjusting the Power Options (PC)

Go to the **Start** button → **Settings** → **Control Panel** → **Display** → **Screen Saver** → **Power...**→ choose the **Power Schemes** tab. Adjust the settings to suit your needs.

Adjusting the Power Options (PC-Laptop)

Go to the Start button → **Settings** → **Control Panel** → **Display** → **Screen Saver** → **Power...**→ choose the **Power Schemes** tab and adjust the settings to suit your needs.

Then, select the **Advanced** tab and customize the settings to suit your needs.

Changing the Screen Resolution (PC)

Go to **Start** → **Settings** → **Control Panel** → **Display** → Choose the **Display** tab → adjust the **Screen resolution** selector to your desired position → click **OK** → You will be given a preview of the new resolution and asked if you would like to keep it. If you like the new resolution click **OK**, if you would like a different resolution click **NO**. You will be taken back to the original resolution. Start the procedure again until you find a suitable resolution.

How to Change the Monitor Resolution (OS X)?

Go to the **Apple icon** → scroll to **System Preferences...**→ click the **Display** icon → after the utility launches adjust the **Resolutions**, **Colors** and **Refresh Rate** to a comfortable level

Changing Screen Resolution (Macintosh OS 9)

Go to the **Apple icon** → go to **Control Panel** → go to **Monitors** and change resolution

SECTION VI. MISCELLANEOUS

What's the difference between JPEG and TIFF files?

TIFF uses a lossless compression process, which means that you will have no loss of detail in the image. Because of its sharpness, TIFF files tend to be large. Use the TIFF format when you plan to print your image. Use **JPEG** if you are going to put your image on the Web or send it via e-mail. While some detail is lost in the compression process using JPEG, it will not be noticeable when viewed on screen, and it provides a compact file size for speedy downloading.

After I was Sent an E-Mail Attachment, The Name Changed To DEFANGED

In an effort to thwart a potential virus or worm, some attachments become unreadable and renamed containing the word **DEFANGED**. The attachment will read something like: filename.12345DEFANGED-html. In effect, the security software disassociates the attachment with the program used to open it, giving you the chance to delete it if necessary. However, if you know the attachment is safe and want to open it, **right-click** the file and select **rename**. For example, if the file is a web page, using the example above, rename the file to **filename.html**. If it is some other program, rename the file as appropriate. **You will usually know the type of extension to use by looking at the letters to the right of DEFANGED**. Below is a list of common extensions and the programs used to read them. The extension would take the place of .html from the example above.

Microsoft Word	.doc
Microsoft Excel	.xls
Microsoft Power Point	.ppt
Microsoft Access	.mdb
Microsoft Publisher	.pub
Microsoft Outlook	.eml
Adobe Acrobat	.pdf
Web Page Links	.html

I Deleted some files from my Hard Drive by mistake

Hopefully, you realized this soon after it happened. The longer you wait the less likely you have of recovering the files, this is true if you continue to save data to the hard drive and/or download new programs. For PCs, however, a company called **Executive Software** makes software called **Undelete** that is capable of restoring deleted files to your computer **before** Undelete was installed. Other software includes **Norton Go Back**, although it may not be able to recover data deleted before installation. There is also a Macintosh version of Norton called **Norton Utilities for Mac**, which contains software called **UnErase**. This software can be used to undelete deleted data and can be used as a start up disk to recover data that had been deleted.

Cleaning Computer Screens

- **LCD Models**

  LCD screens should be cleaned with a soft cloth or paper towel moistened with water. Using glass cleaners can cause the screen to become cloudy over time. In addition, using a hard or rough cloth or paper towel can scratch the screen.

- **CRT Models**

  Glass-plated CRT monitors can be cleaned with a glass cleaner using either a paper-towel or soft cloth.

How do I delete a file when a message says the file is locked (OS 9 and OS X)

Hold down the **Option** key while selecting **Empty Trash** from the **Special** menu

or

Unlock the file first: Press and hold the **ctrl (Control)** key → **single-click** on the file you are trying to delete → open the **Get Info** dialog box → select **General Information** → *uncheck* the **Locked** check box in the lower-left corner.

Mac cannot access the network. (OS 9)

- Is the Ethernet cable plugged into the correct port?

- Re-seat the cable at both ends—wall port and computer.

- Go to **Apple icon** → **Control Panels** and select **AppleTalk**. In the **Connect via** menu, select **Ethernet**—also called Ethernet Built-in.

- If Ethernet is not an option, but the Mac has an Ethernet port, move the AppleTalk Preferences file to the trash. (**Hard Drive Icon** → **System Folder** → **Preferences** → **AppleTalk Preferences**) → **restart** your Mac.

- Next, go to the **Apple icon** → **Control Panels** → select **TCP/IP** → In the **Connect via** menu select **Ethernet** → From the **Configure** pop-up menu, select **DHCP**.

- If this doesn't work, **zap** the **PRAM** (Restart the computer → press **Command (Apple Key)-Option-P-R**, hold down the keys for three consecutive Apple Startup chimes then release the keys.

Configuring your Mac's Network Preferences (OS X)

- Go to the **Apple icon** → scroll to **System Preferences** → select **Network** → select the **Location** pull-down → choose **Automatic** → From the **Show** pull-down menu, select **Built-in Ethernet** → From the **Configure** pull-down menu choose **Using DHCP**

- Click on the **AppleTalk** tab → check the box **Make AppleTalk Active** → From the **Configure** Pull-down box within the AppleTalk Tab → choose **Automatically** → Click

Apply Now → **Proxies** tab to insure that no proxies are checked or configured → Click **Apply Now** to save these settings.

Configuring your PC's Network Settings (PC)

Right-click the **My Network Places** icon → scroll to **Properties** → Right-click **Local Area Connection (LAN)** → Make sure the following are installed and checked:

1. **Client for Microsoft Networks**

2. **File and Printer Sharing for Microsoft Networks**

3. **Internet Protocol (TCP/IP)**

Single-click **Internet Protocol (TCP/IP)** → click **Properties** → Make sure **Obtain an IP address automatically (DHCP)** is selected → **Obtain DNS server addresses automatically** should be selected as well → Click **OK**.

Why does my hard drive capacity appear to be smaller than what I ordered?

Hard drive manufacturers always quote the capacity of their disk drives in units based on thousands, millions, and billions of bytes (1 Kb = 1024 bytes).

A 40GB unformatted (blank) drive would have the following formatted capacity:

40,000,000,000 bytes/1024 = 39,062,500 Kb
39,062,500 KB/1024 = 38,147 MB
38,147 MB/1024 = 37.29 GB

Therefore, a 40GB hard drive would equal roughly 37.29GB after it is formatted since file allocation tables and other system data take up space.

gigabyte	=	1,024MB
terabyte	=	1,024GB
petabyte	=	1,024TB
exabyte	=	1,024PB
zettabyte	=	1,024EB
yottabyte	=	1,024ZB

Closing or Minimize all open Windows at Once (PC)

If you have many applications that you want to close at once, hold down the **Ctrl** key and click on the application you want to close on the **taskbar** (the bar at the bottom of your screen), **right-click** one of the applications, a context menu will appear for you to Close, Minimize or Maximize. Select one action and all the applications you selected will close, minimize or maximize at the same time.

Accessing Apple's BSD Unix

To access Apple's Unix shell go to the **Hard Drive** icon → **Applications** → **Utilities** → and double-click the **Terminal** icon. This will launch the Unix Shell (Shell prompt). Once the shell is launched, you will be able to use many of the same Shell Prompt commands found in the Linux section of this book.

Enabling OS X Root Account

By default, Apple ships their computers with the root account disabled. This is probably due to the fact that the root account has unrestricted access to the computer and the possibly to inadvertently delete an important system file or folder increases as root. However, when using the shell prompt many commands require that you become root (*su-*). As long s you know what you are doing, delete as little as possible and consult the *man* pages when in doubt, you should be okay while rooting around.

NOTE: The order varies depending on the OS X version

Go to the **Hard Drive** icon → **Applications** → **Utilities** → **NetInfo Manager** → **Domain** → **Security** → **Authenticate** → **Enable Root User** → type in the computer's administrator password when prompted, if none leave the space blank and click **OK** → you will be prompted for a root account password and click **OK**. Root account is now created. **Exit** NetInfo Manager.

You will now be able to login as root. You will also be able to start a shell prompt as root even when logged in as another user, to do start the Terminal and at the prompt type su—then type the password when prompted. You are now using BSD Unix as root.

SECTION VII. PROBLEMS AND DIAGNOSTIC TOOLS

How to Defragment(Defrag) the Hard Drive (PC)

Defragmenting the hard drive helps to organize all of the files, folders, and programs on your computer. Defragmenting can significantly increase the performance of a computer. Defragment your hard drive at least once a month, particularly if you save a lot of data to your hard drive. **Be sure to turn off screen savers and power saving modes so that the defragmenting can run uninterrupted.**

Double-click the **My Computer** icon → **right-click** the **C:** (or other drive you wish to defrag) → scroll to **Properties** → select the **Tools** tab → click **Defragment Now...**→ click **Defragment.** This process may take up to 30-minutes—depending on the severity of fragmentation.

How to Defragment the Hard Drive (OS 9 and OS X)

There is no built-in defragmentation utility for OS 9.x and OS X. You will need to buy a third-party utility such as Norton System Works and perform a **disk optimization**.

How to Run a Hard Drive Diagnostic (PC)

Sometimes a hard drive finds that it's hard to drive. During these times strange error codes appear that not even the veteran troubleshooter can understand. A technique to use to check out the hard drive include running a hard drive diagnostic. To run this built-in diagnostic start up the computer and press these keys together **ALT + Ctrl+ D.**
NOTE: This utility may not work on all computer systems.

Another built-in Windows utility you can use is the **chkdsk** utility. To run it, go to the **command prompt** and type **chkdsk** or **chkdsk/F.**

How to Run a System Diagnostic (Mac OS 9)

Go to **the Apple icon** → go to **Applications (Mac OS9)** folder → **Utilities** → **Disk First Aid** → in the **Select Volumes to verify:** box click the hard drive you wish to check → click the **Repair** button.

How to Run a System Diagnostic (OS X)

Go to the Hard Drive icon → go to **Utilities** → go to **Disk Utility** → **in the left column select the disk you wish to check** → in the right column click the **Repair Disk** button.
NOTE: You may need to use an OS X startup disk. Contact Apple for help.

What to do when I get an error saying either: "Non system disk error" or "Disk error" or "Can't find NTLdr"?

Remove any floppy disks or Zip disks from the computer. If there are none, the operating system may need to be checked or re-installed. Additionally, your hard drive may be damaged.

How to Force-Quit Stubborn Applications (PC)

1. Simultaneously press **Shift, Ctrl, Esc**—or—**Alt, Ctrl, Delete**
2. Click the **Applications** tab → select the program that is no longer responding.
3. Click **End Task**.

How to Force-Quit Stubborn Applications (OS 9 and OS X)

When an application stops responding you can easily force quit the application by a few keystrokes. Press the **Apple** key (also called the **Command** key), together with the **Option** key and the **esc** key. Select the application that is having the problem and press **Force Quit**

What to do when my PC has a blue screen with a message saying: "Performing Dump of Physical Memory"?

Restart your computer or uninstall newly added hardware or software. Problems could be bad memory, not enough memory or issues with newly installed hardware or software. Contact your computer manufacturer if the problem persists. If all else fails, it may be time to reinstall the operating system.

How to start-up OS X in Command-line to check and Repair Disk Errors (OS X)

Restart the computer → Immediately after the startup sound, **press and hold both the Command (Apple) and "s" keys** → The computer will display a series of text messages, at which time you may release these keys.

When the computer has started up, it will display a command line prompt (#). The computer is now in single-user mode.

At the prompt (#), type:**/sbin/fsck** → Press **Return**.

The fsck utility will go through five "phases" and then return information about the disk's utilization and fragmentation. Once the check is finished, if no issue is found, you should see ** **The volume <name of volume> appears to be OK**.

If fsck alters, repairs, or fixes anything, it will display the message:

***** FILE SYSTEM WAS MODIFIED *****

Important: If this message appears, repeat with the**/sbin/fsck-y** command until this message no longer appears. It is normal for your computer to require several fsck to uncover additional errors.

When fsck has completed type **reboot** → press **Return**. The computer should start-up normally.

When the Mac won't start (OS 9.x)

If your Mac Freezes during the start-up process or displays a flashing question mark or a "Sad Mac" icon Steps to take include:

- **Try zapping the PRAM.**

  Restart the computer → press **Command-Option-P-R** → hold down the keys for three consecutive Apple Start-up chimes then release the keys.

- If the computer starts up → run **Disk First Aid** to diagnose any problems. If Disk First Aid cannot repair the problems, try booting from and external device and running **TechTool Pro** to examine and/or repair the drive.

- If TechTool Pro repairs the drive but the Mac still won't boot, **Reinstall or Upgrade the System Software** (upgrade OS 9.1 to OS 9.2).

When To Update Your System

If you have exhausted all other options—that include running system and third-party disk utility programs, it may be time to re-install or upgrade the operating system. The last resort is formatting the hard drive which erases everything and allows you to start from scratch.

The following pages contain information on basic to advanced techniques to perform when experiencing operating system problems. Techniques include how to re-install an operating system, how to upgrade an operating system and finally how to format the hard drive. Before performing such techniques, be sure to **back up your important data** to an external storage device.

Section VIII. Upgrading, Re-installing and Formatting

Upgrading Your Operating System

Important, before upgrading or formatting the hard drive, be sure to back up all of your important data to a CD/DVD or other external device.

Using a PC

On the surface, upgrading your operating system involves installing a new user interface. Under the surface, however, upgrading installs new system files to help the computer run more efficiently, faster, support more hardware, better manage system security and allows your computing experience to be more pleasing from start up to shut down. There are two common ways in which to upgrade your operating system, one way is to do an **in-place upgrade** another is to do a **clean install**.

The **in-place re-install** is the simplest and less thorough upgrade to perform. The steps are relatively straightforward. However, the person performing the upgrade must have administrative rights on the computer:

- Start your computer as usual and go to the desktop.

- Insert the disk containing the operating system.

- The new system disk should automatically prompt you that disk contains a new operating system and if you wish to reinstall the current system.

- From here you should be able to follow the prompts and successfully install the system on your own, using all of the default settings provided.

- Once the installer has completed, the fresh version of the operating system will be installed. After restarting the computer, you should be able to experience a better functioning operating system.

With an in-place re-install, all of the programs installed on the system and all of the files, folders and documents that were previously installed on the system will remain. Additionally, they should all work fine after the re-install. However, there are some instances where some programs may need to be re-installed in order to function properly.

NOTE: Downgrading of the operating system—or installing an operating system that is older than the one already installed—will not work.

The **clean install** is a more advanced technique used to re-install or upgrade an operating system. This technique is more involved and usually deletes all of the contents on the hard drive. The person performing the clean install should be an administrator of the computer.

- Start your computer as usual and go to the desktop.

- Insert the disk containing the operating system.

- The new system disk should automatically prompt you that the disk contains a new operating system and if you wish to upgrade, or reinstall the current system.

- From here you should be able to follow the prompts and successfully install the system on your own, using all of the default settings provided.

- Once the installer has completed, the new operating system will be installed. After restarting the computer, you will be able to experience the new interface of the upgraded operating system.

With a clean install upgrade, all of the programs installed on the system and all of the files, folders and documents that were previously installed will be deleted.

Using a Mac OS 9

Apple makes re-installing the operating system a quick and easy process. When re-installing, all files, programs and folders are kept intact. Only a few system preferences are changed which can be easily corrected. Whether performing a system upgrade or restore-in-place install, most of the files and programs will remain intact.

- Start the computer as usual and go to the desktop
- Insert the disk containing the operating system
- The installer should automatically open
- Double-click the Install OS icon
- Answer "yes" to have the computer automatically restart and install, or upgrade the operating system
- Follow and answer the prompts that are asked
- System will be upgraded

Using a Mac OS X

Apple has based the OS X operating system on Unix. However, when performing clean installations or restore-in-place upgrades, problems tend to occur with permissions when attempting to access previously installed files, folders and documents.

- Start the computer as usual and go to the desktop
- Insert the disk containing the operating system
- The installer should automatically open
- Double-click the Install OS icon
- Answer "yes" to have the computer automatically restart and install, or upgrade the operating system
- Follow and answer the prompts that are asked

- System will be upgraded

Formatting the hard drive

Formatting wipes out everything on the hard drive. It prepares the drive to accept a new operating system which can sometimes fix major operating system problems. Formatting is also advisable to delete all of the contents of the hard drive before selling or disposing of the computer. **Remember to back up your data before formatting the hard drive**.

Using a PC

- Insert the CD containing the operating system

- Restart the computer

- After restarting, CD should spin-up and load the image and you should get a message that says: **Press any key to boot from CD...**

- Press any key on the keyboard

- Follow the prompts and agree to the agreements

- Follow the on-screen instructions and delete the installed Windows partitions

- Confirm and delete the partitions, **all the data will be lost**

- If you wish to Partition—divide—the hard drive, choose the size of your partitions, if not, proceed to the next step.

- When asked about formatting, choose **Format the Partition using NTFS** (choose **Quick Install** if using Windows XP) NTFS is a better file system for saving and encrypting data. Hard drives of 40GB or more will only have NTFS as a choice.

- **Before proceeding you can press Cancel if you change your mind and nothing will be lost**. Otherwise, proceeding will start the formatting process and your hard drive will be erased.

If your computer does not prompt you at startup to **Press any key to boot from CD...**follow the steps below.

- Insert the CD containing the operating system

- Restart the computer

- Press **F2** to go into the BIOS (check with your computer vendor for appropriate key combinations to get into the BIOS)

- Scroll to the tab indicating **Boot (or Boot Order)**

- Using the instructions found at the bottom of the BIOS screen, change the order so that the CD-ROM drive is the first boot device.

- Using the instructions found at the bottom of the BIOS screen, save the changes and exit.

- The computer should then be able to start up from the CD and the **Press any key to boot from CD…**should prompt you.

If you are still not able to start the computer from the CD, and you are using an older model of computer, the computer may not be able to boot from a CD. In this case, you will have to use floppy disks to complete the first stages of the installation. But first, you must create a boot disk.

Windows 95/98/NT

Step 1. Create a boot disk (4 blank floppy disks needed for NT)

1. Click Start → Settings → Control Panel
2. Click on Add/Remove Programs
3. Select Startup Disk tab → click Create Disk
4. Insert disk and click OK
5. Once information has been written to disk click OK and remove disk

Step 2. Format the hard drive

1. Restart the computer, keeping the newly created disk inside
2. Once the Computer starts up, you will see **a:**
3. Type in format c: (*e.g. format c:*)
4. When asked "Do you really want to do this?" press enter and the formatting will take place
5. When formatting has completed, you will be prompted "Do you want to put a label name on the disk?" Press enter
6. The system will return to a:\ prompt, from here you can install the new operating system. See Step 3 of the Windows 2000 section below.

Windows 2000

Step 1. Create a Boot disk (4 blank floppy disks needed)

1. Insert your Windows 2000 CD, double-click the My Computer icon
2. Right-click the CD ROM drive and select Browse This CD
3. Open the Bootdisk folder
4. Double-click the Makeboot icon
5. At the Command Prompt type the letter of your floppy drive, (*e.g. a:*)
6. Insert a blank floppy disk
7. Windows will copy files to the disks. (You will need 4 blank floppy disks. Be sure to label the disks).

Step 2. Format the hard drive

1. Restart the computer with disk 1 inserted

2. When asked, "Do you want to repair or install Windows 2000?" choose yes and press enter

3. When prompted, "You already have a Windows partition. Do you want to delete the partition?" choose yes.

4. Choose yes when prompted, "Do you want to create a partition?"

5. Choose yes when prompted, "Do you want to format the partition?"

6. Formatting will begin. Once completed press F3, then quit or restart the computer. The computer will then be ready for you to install the new operating system.

NOTE: You can also use the format disk to format a hard drive on which Linux is installed.

That should be all that is needed for the hard drive formatting process. Go to the Microsoft downloads web site for the specific Windows XP boot disks that matches your installation, or go to http://bootdisk.com/bootdisk.htm

Step 3. Installing the Operating system

- Insert the appropriate floppy disk

- Restart the computer

- You should get the prompt to **Press any key to boot from CD...**(if you still do not get this message follow the next step involving the BIOS)

- Go into the BIOS and change the boot order so that the Floppy Drive is the first device

- Save the changes and exit

- Try starting from the floppy disk again.

Using a Mac OS X

Formatting a hard drive under the Macintosh operating system allows for a detailed process called the **zero all data** method. This method permanently erases all data and writes zeroes to the hard drives to make any recovery attempt less possible, and supposedly fixes many unforeseen problems that may have been on the previous system. Depending on the size of the hard drive, this zeroing process is quite lengthy, taking anywhere from two hours to four hours. The process of zeroing all data is described below.

- Insert the Mac OS X CD.

- Restart the computer.

- Press and hold the C key while the computer starts.

- When the Installer screen appears, look across the top of the screen and choose Installer
- Go to Open Disk Utilities
- Select the hard drive to erase
- Click the Erase tab
- Click Options button
- Check Zero all data
- Click OK
- Click Erase.

Using Mac OS 9

- Insert the OS 9 Install CD
- Restart the computer
- Press and hold the C key while the computer starts
- OS 9 from the disk will load
- Double-Click the CD icon
- Double-Click the Utilities Folder
- Double-Click Drive Setup
- Select the Hard drive by clicking it once
- Select Initialization Options from the Function Menu
- Check Zero all data
- Click OK
- Click Initialize
- Once the format process has completed, the operating system will install.

	In Place Upgrade	Clean Install	Format
Uses	Reinstalls a faulty operating system Fixes minor problems	Reinstalls a faulty operating system Fixes minor problems and system annoyances Can upgrade an existing operating system	Completely wipes out data on a faulty operating system Fixes major problems Destroys data from the hard drive before computer is sold, donated or recycled
Advantages	Quick Data Loss is less likely	Slightly longer than an in place install Data loss is Less likely on a Mac	Completely destroys data from the hard drive Often corrects problems with the operating system and hardware The computer can often experience better performance
Disadvantages	May not fix all the operating system problems	May not fix all the operating system problems On PCs, software must be reinstalled	Lengthy Process Recovery of data is less possible if you find you did not remove some important data All system software, hardware (drivers), and previous files must be reinstalled

25

Recycling

Recycling—Where to Recycle Your Old Computer and Printer Equipment

You can take your personal computer equipment and printers to be recycled at specific recycling locations in your area. Although **Goodwill** and **The Salvation Army** will accept working computers, monitors and printers, the links listed below offer comprehensive information for recycling and/or donating computer and printer equipment.

http://www.svtc.org/cleancc/recycle/recycletable.html This site has a list of destinations where you can take your old computer equipment to be recycled in the San Francisco Bay Area.

http://www.nsc.org/ehc/epr2/DONATE.HTM This site has good general information about proper recycling and donating your used computer equipment for tax breaks. They will pay the shipping fees, too.

http://sharetechnology.org/cartridges.html This site has good information for recycling your used inkjet printer cartridges.

Happy Computing.

Index

0-595-30915-1